A. Bromley Crane

Facts of faith

Or first lessons in christianity

A. Bromley Crane

Facts of faith
Or first lessons in christianity

ISBN/EAN: 9783742861290

Manufactured in Europe, USA, Canada, Australia, Japa

Cover: Foto ©Lupo / pixelio.de

Manufactured and distributed by brebook publishing software (www.brebook.com)

A. Bromley Crane

Facts of faith

FACTS OF FAITH:

OR

FIRST LESSONS IN CHRISTIANITY.

COMPILED BY

The Rev. A. Bromley Crane,

Of St. Wilfrid's College, Cotton, Cheadle.

Permissu Superiorum.

LEAMINGTON: ART AND BOOK COMPANY.
LONDON: BURNS AND OATES.
NEW YORK: CATHOLIC PUBLICATION SOCIETY COMPANY.

STRATFORD-ON-AVON :

PRINTED AT ST GREGORY'S PRESS.

1885.

CONTENTS.

CHAPTER.		PAGE.
I.	THE GROUNDWORK OF FAITH	1
II.	THE APOSTLES' CREED	10
III.	HOPE AND PRAYER	63
IV.	CHARITY	72
V.	THE DECALOGUE	78
VI.	THE SEVEN SACRAMENTS	108
VII.	THE PRECEPTS OF THE CHURCH	174
VIII.	THE CHRISTIAN LIFE	178

CHAPTER I.

THE GROUNDWORK OF FAITH.

1. God and the Soul.—There is one God Almighty, whose existence our reason makes known to us.

He is known to our reason as the Creator of all things, and as the Rewarder of good and the Punisher of evil.

"For the invisible things of Him (His eternal power and divinity) from the creation of the world are clearly seen, being perceived through the things that are made" (Rom. i. 20).

For the stars above and the earth beneath, the flowers and herbs and trees, each kind with its use and beauty, the insects, animals, birds and fishes, all living things with their various natures and needful instincts, and most of all, man, with his reason and conscience, and inborn sense of right and wrong— all these things proclaim that their Maker was a Being of infinite power and wisdom and righteousness, that is, GOD.

Reason also tells us—That man has a soul, which feels and thinks and governs his body;

That the soul, unlike the body, is one and indivisible, that is, is not composed of parts that can be separated one from another;

And that therefore the soul will never die; for death is dissolution or the separation of parts.

Moreover everywhere, and even among people that could never have reasoned these things out, there has been found a belief in the existence of God, a belief in the immortality of the soul, and a belief that good deeds will be rewarded and bad deeds punished, not so much here as in future life.

And God has revealed that these beliefs are true.

They are therefore truths of *reason*, truths of *universal tradition*, and lastly truths of *faith*.

2. Revelation.—God has never left human reason entirely to itself to argue out the great truths of religion.

For the very first man was favoured with various revelations of the presence and the will of God.

And though almost all the races of men corrupted, as time went on, the tradition of the primeval revelations, and plunged themselves deeper and deeper into ignorance and crime, yet God had always on the earth one faithful family at least who kept alive the Divine Tradition.

To this family He manifested Himself from time to time: at one time preserving Noah and his children amid the waters of the deluge; at another calling Abraham, and saying,—"I will make of thee a great nation, . . . and in thee shall all the kindred of the earth be blessed;" repeating the promise to Isaac,—"In thy seed shall all the nations of the earth be blessed;" and again to Jacob,—"In thee and in thy seed shall all the tribes of the earth be blessed;" and again by the lips of the dying Jacob to Judah,—"The sceptre shall not be taken away from Judah . . . . until He come who shall be sent, and He shall be the expectation of the nations" (Gen. xii. 2, 3; xxvi. 4; xxviii. 14; xlix. 10).

Later on, when the children of Israel or Jacob were a mighty people indeed in point of numbers, but had been for long years in Egyptian bondage, God delivered them by the hand of Moses, brought them to Mount Sinai, gave them the law, and made a Covenant or agreement with them that as long as they observed His holy law, He would be their God and they should be His people. (Lev. xxvi. 12).

3. The Expectation of the Messiah.—The Jews were therefore a chosen race—a people with a destiny—a people that lived for a national hope and expectation.

That hope looked forward to a man that was to come, a prophet like unto Moses (Deut. xviii. 15), and to a new Covenant.

"Behold the days shall come, saith the Lord, and I will make a new Covenant with the house of Israel and with the house of Judah" (Jeremias xxxi. 31).

Other prophets enlarged upon this theme and added details to the prophecy, till at last the Jewish people had fixed the very time for the coming of the Christ or the Messias.

And at that very time He came.

4. Jesus Christ gave proof, by the conspicuous and surpassing purity of His life, by the evident holiness of His doctrine, by His miracles, and by the fulfilment in His person of many ancient prophecies, that he came from God and was indeed "The Prophet" foretold by Moses (Deut. xviii. 15), the expectation of the nations, the promised Messias.

So "He taught as one having authority" (Matt. vii. 29), as one sent by God the Father (Luke iv. 18; John xx. 21), and as the Son of God (John x. 37).

He explained the Old Testament Scriptures.

He gave out anew all the truth they contained.

He revealed many hitherto unknown facts about God, and His attributes, and His will, and what things please Him and what things offend Him.

And He showed Himself the perfect pattern, as well as the teacher, of every virtue.

The religion He taught is now called Christianity.

5. The Christian Religion.—All the revelations that God has made of Himself and His will, and all the moral truth that is known by reason and conscience, are gathered up, incorporated, harmonised and completed in the religion of Jesus Christ.

And so, Christianity, when compared with other religious systems, manifestly excels them all.

It excels them in the extent, coherence, and purity of its teaching about God;

It excels them in its perfect knowledge of man's nature and his moral and even physical needs;

And it excels them in its morality, that is, (1) in its account of God's moral conduct towards man, and (2) in its moral precepts for the guidance of man's conduct towards God and towards his fellow men.

And this manifest excellence of Christianity is in turn a proof that Christianity is not an imposture, but a genuine message from God.

6. The Christian Church.—The Divine Founder of Christianity did not write His doctrines and His moral precepts in a book and cast it out into the world, without authorised exponent or interpreter, to be a riddle to after ages.

In other words He did not commit His doctrine to "the Bible and the Bible only," nor make an Inspired Volume the one organ of His revelation.

He spent the three years and more of His public life, not in writing a book, but in impressing His doctrines, His spirit, His principles (so to speak) upon the minds of a number of living men.

To some few of these, whom He called His Apostles, He took care to make known the whole of His doctrine, "whatsoever" He had "heard from the Father" (John xv. 15).

Then, as the Father had sent Him to preach the Gospel (Luke iv. 18), He gave the same mission to his Apostles; "as the Father hath sent Me," He said, "I also send you," (John xx. 21); that is, He sent them "to teach (or make disciples of) all nations" Matt. xviii. 19).

And He promised them the Holy Ghost the Spirit of Truth to abide with them for ever (John xiv. 16), to teach them all things and to bring all His words to their remembrance (John xiv. 26), and to guide them in all truth (John xvi. 13).

That is, He established a Teaching Church, or a corporate body of teachers, and charged them in His name to teach ALL nations to observe ALL His commandments ALL days even to the end of the world.

7. Christian and Catholic.—Christianity unmutilated, and in the perfection of its growth and development, is Roman Catholicism.

For the Catholic Church and the Catholic Religion of the nineteenth century are the Christian Church and the Christian Religion of the first.

The continuity of the Catholic Church is unbroken from the time when it was planted by Christ like a seed (Matt. xiii. 31) even to the nineteenth century, when it appears as a full-grown tree, spreading its branches over all the world.

It has the same organisation and hierarchy now as it received from Christ.

Its line of Chief Pastors is one and unbroken from St. Peter, the first Pope, on whom the Church was founded (Matt. xvi. 18), to Leo XIII, the 258th Pope, now happily reigning.

And it worships God by the same holy Sacrifice, the Mass; it points out the same way to heaven, the way of the commandments; and it offers to all the same means of grace, the sacraments, now, as it has done in every age.

In short, *because* it is the Church of Christ, *therefore* it teaches His doctrine; teaches it fully, and teaches it clearly; for being in all ages the Body of Christ (Eph. i. 8, 23) its voice is in every age the voice of God.

8. The Old and New Testament.—Nevertheless, God has willed that there should be in the world a written testimony of Himself, of His revelations and of His law.

In time past therefore He inspired holy men to write the books of the Old Testament.

And after the foundation of Christianity He inspired several of the Apostles and their disciples to write, at divers times and places, the books of the New Testament, or the Christian Scriptures.

The New Testament Scriptures do not pretend to give a complete account of the Christian Religion, nor to set forth in order the whole doctrine of Christ.

Yet they tell us quite enough of our Blessed Lord's teaching to enable us to identify that teaching with the teaching of the Catholic Church; they imply many truths, as for example about the nature and effects of the sacraments, which are clearly and fully made known to us only by the traditional teaching of the Church; and, above all, the four Gospels tell us almost all the facts we know about the life and death of our Redeemer.

The Scriptures therefore are, so to speak, the title-deeds of the Christian Church.

9. The Way of Salvation.—The ordinary way of salvation lies in the Catholic Church.

For though our Lord has sheep that "are not of this Fold," yet "them also," He says, "I must bring, and they shall hear my voice; and there shall be One Fold and One Shepherd" (John x. 16).

This then is man's whole duty: to belong to the Flock, or Church of Christ, and to walk in His Church by the way of His holy law.

And this is His law, which none can disobey without incurring His anger:—

(1) That we believe in God and in Jesus Christ His Son, and in all the truths He has revealed;

(2) That we hope for life everlasting, trust in the goodness of God and in the merits and promises of Christ, and earnestly pray for grace to save our souls;

(3) That we love God more than all things, do good works to please Him, keep His commandments,

renounce all pleasure or gain which they forbid, and so take up our cross and follow Christ.

In short, we must worship God by Faith, Hope, and Charity, and by the outward expression of these virtues, at proper times and seasons, in acts of Religion.

And to do all this rightly we must needs be members of the Church; for only in the Church, which is the "pillar and ground of the truth" (1 Tim. iii. 15), can we know revealed truth in its fulness, have the aid and grace of all the sacraments, and obtain the full benefit of the Communion of Saints.

10. Divine Faith.—Faith means belief in something which is told us, and which we know to be true, not because we can see it, or can prove it, but because it is told us by some one else.

Divine Faith means belief in truths, which we cannot see, or prove to be true, but which God has revealed.

The perfection of Divine Faith is to believe without doubting whatever the Catholic Church teaches.

For the Church is commissioned to teach what God has revealed;

And what God has revealed is infallibly true;

For God is Truth.

God's truthfulness or veracity is therefore the motive of Catholic Faith, or our reason for believing what the Catholic Church teaches.

And therefore an act of Faith, being an act of homage paid to God's veracity, is an act of Divine worship.

11. The Necessity of Faith.—To believe in revealed truth is a condition of salvation.

For our Blessed Lord has said "He that believeth not shall be condemned" (Mak xvi. 16);

And St. Paul has added, "Without Faith it is impossible to please God" (Heb xi. 6).

All men are therefore bound to believe whatever they know to have been in any way revealed by God.

Some men may have only the light of reason to guide them; but even these, by the grace of Him "who enlighteneth every man that cometh into this world" (John i. 9), may know at least that God is, and that He is the Rewarder of good and evil.

Others, as those brought up amongst Jews and heretics, may have reason and grace, (1) to believe in detail many revealed truths that are plainly taught in Scripture, and (2) to believe many more truths implicitly, if they believe that whatever Scripture teaches is true.

Such men as these are bound to believe according to their knowledge; and they are also bound to increase their knowledge, as soon as they become conscious of its defectiveness.

And, lastly, those who have means of knowing that the Christian Church is the divinely appointed teacher of truth, are bound to believe that all things whatsoever, pertaining to salvation, which God has made known to the Church, either by direct revelation, as the mystery of the Incarnation, or by natural means providentially employed, as the facts of sacred history, are true.

And they are bound to know and to believe those truths in detail, one by one, so far as they need to know them in order to do God's will and to save their souls.

The obligation of Faith is not difficult to comply with; for Faith is a gift of God.

That is, all men are moved and assisted by grace to believe what God has taught

And especially to Christians there is given at their baptism a permanent power, disposition and inclination to believe, which is called the Infused Virtue of Faith.

And the virtue of Faith remains in the soul until it is destroyed by some contrary mortal sin, that is, wilful doubt or disbelief.

12. False Religions.—All faiths are false but that of Christ.

All other religions but that revealed by him are fragmentary, and false wherever they differ from His.

All churches are spurious and unchristian (however sincere and morally good their members may be) but that one Church which Christ Himself established.

No apostate monk like Luther, no profligate king like Henry VIII, no perjured queen like Elizabeth, no man nor woman on earth, nor even an angel from heaven, can set up a church against that which Jesus built on Peter, or preach a gospel other than that which Jesus gave to his Apostles, without being *anathema*, or accursed (Gal. i. 8, 9).

So no sect founded by Luther, or Calvin, or Henry VIII, or Queen Elizabeth, or Wesley, or the Countess of Huntingdon, or any other man or woman, can be *the* Church or Flock of Christ, or any part or "branch" of it.

And so the ministers of such sects, however well-intentioned they may nowadays be, not being heirs to the promises of Christ nor having the Spirit of Truth for their guide, misunderstand the Scripture, corrupt the Gospel, and in many things deceive the people, and lead them to disobey God.

But how far the people, and even many ministers, are really deceived; how little individuals are answerable for their own disobedience; how many obtain God's grace by their baptism, faith and good works; how many sin, or do not sin, against the light; how many follow their conscience and act up to Gospel Truth so far as they know it; how many are thus in the way of salvation through their partial acquaintance with Gospel Truth and in spite of their Protestant errors, are secrets known to God alone.

13. The True Religion, on the other hand, or the right way of knowing, loving, serving, and worshipping God, is the Religion taught by Jesus

Christ—the Religion of His One, Holy, Catholic, Apostolic and Roman Church.

This Religion is founded upon certain definite truths, some known to the natural reason, and some divinely revealed: namely, facts about God, His nature, character and three-fold personality; about man, his destiny, sin and fallen state; about the Incarnation, life and death of Christ, and His Redemption of the human race; about the Holy Ghost and grace; about the Church and its prerogatives; about the Sacraments; about the future life; and about the virtues which form the Christian character.

These truths are summarised in the Apostles' Creed, and may be briefly explained as follows.

CHAPTER II.
THE APOSTLES' CREED.

14. The Apostles' Creed.—A Creed is an authentic summary of truths to be believed, and is used as a profession of faith, or a declaration that we believe in truths revealed by God.

There are four Creeds used in the Church—the Apostles' Creed, the Nicene Creed, the Athanasian Creed, and the Creed of Pope Pius IV.

The oldest of these is the Apostles' Creed, which runs as follows, and is usually divided into twelve parts or articles:—

   I. I believe in God, the Father Almighty, Creator of heaven and earth;
   II. And in Jesus Christ, His only Son, our Lord;
   III. Who was conceived by the Holy Ghost, born of the Virgin Mary;
   IV. Suffered under Pontius Pilate, was crucified, dead, and buried;

V. He descended into hell; the third day He rose again from the dead;
VI. He ascended into heaven; sitteth at the right hand of God the Father Almighty;
VII. From thence He shall come to judge the living and the dead.
VIII. I believe in the Holy Ghost;
IX. The Holy Catholic Church; the Communion of Saints;
X. The forgiveness of sins;
XI. The resurrection of the body;
XII. And life everlasting. Amen.

FIRST ARTICLE OF THE CREED.

I believe in God, the Father Almighty, Creator of heaven and earth.

15. God and His Attributes.—There is one true and living God.

God exists of Himself.

He has lived from all eternity in the past, and He will live for ever in the future.

He had no beginning; He will have no end.

He always was, He is, and He always will be.

God is everywhere.

We cannot see God because He is a *spirit;* that is, He is a Being that lives and thinks and acts, but has no body.

But God sees *us*, and knows our very thoughts.

God knows all things—how many hairs there are on our heads, how many leaves on the trees, how many good deeds we do and how many bad ones.

He knows all that has happened in days gone by, and all that will happen in days to come.

He is Almighty, that is, all-powerful, able to do all things.

He is wise; He knows what good to do, and how to do it.

He is good—good in Himself and good to us.

He is holy, and He hates all wickedness with an everlasting hatred.

He takes care of all by His Providence, and gives to us all the means to save our souls.

God is Truth. Whatever He tells us is true, and whatever He promises He will certainly perform.

He loves His creatures, and earnestly wishes all men to be saved.

Such then is God; for such He *must* be, being God; and such He is said to be in hundreds of places in Holy Scripture.

God's Power, Knowledge, Wisdom, Goodness, &c., are called His Attributes or Perfections.

And because He has in Himself all Power, all Knowledge, all Wisdom, all Goodness; or rather because He *is* Power, Knowledge, Wisdom, Goodness, and whatever else is good; He is said to be Infinite, that is, without end or limit, in all Perfections.

16. The Blessed Trinity.—God is a Trinity, that is, Three-in-One.

In God there are three persons, God the Father, God the Son, and God the Holy Ghost.

The Father is the first person, the Son is the second person, and the Holy Ghost is the third person.

God the Father exists, unborn, unmade.

God the Son is born of the Father from all eternity.

God the Holy Ghost proceeds from the Father and the Son together, being the eternal love of both.

The Father, the Son and the Holy Ghost are all one and the same God, and have all the same wisdom, goodness, power and glory, being equal to each other in all things.

But observe, God is not One in the same sense as He is Three. He is One in His nature, substance or essence; He is Three in person only.

Nevertheless, how this can be we cannot understand. It is a mystery, that is, a truth revealed by God and known through faith, but beyond the power of our reason to comprehend.

17. Creator of heaven and earth.—That the world must have had a Creator, and that that Creator could be God alone, are truths which Christian philosophers have proved to demonstration.

But long before they proved them, God Himself had revealed them; for the first words of Scripture are,— "In the beginning God created heaven and earth" (Gen. I. i).

He made them and all that is in them in six days, and He made them out of nothing. "He spoke and they were made; He commanded and they were created" (Ps. cxlviii. 5).

It is God the Father who is called the "Creator of heaven and earth," because He is so in a special sense; yet it was not the Father alone that created, but Father, Son and Holy Ghost together.

The history of the creation is briefly told in the first chapter of Genesis.

18. Heaven.—In heaven God made nine choirs, or kinds, of angels.

The angels are spirits; they are living beings that have free will, great power, great knowledge, and intelligence, but have no bodies like ours.

God, when He made them, gave them grace to make them holy, and thus fitted them to love Him and serve Him, and to be His friends, His ministers and messengers. The word *angel* means *messenger* or *servant*.

In all probability God created the angels when He created the world, and their numbers are probably millions upon millions (see Dan. vii. 10).

19. The fall of Lucifer.—Some of the angels sinned and fell from their state of grace.

Their sin is believed to have been an act of pride.

The chief of the proud and rebellious angels was Lucifer (Isaias xiv. 12), who is now called the devil, Satan, or the Dragon.

"God spared not the angels that sinned: but delivered them drawn down by infernal ropes to the lower hell," &c. (2 Peter, ii. 4). And this lower hell "prepared for the devil and his angels" is "everlasting fire" (Matt. xxv. 41).

The devil and his angels, though burning in hell, have power to tempt us to sin; and have sometimes had power to torment and to possess the bodies of men.

20. The good Angels are those that did not sin.

They now "see the face" of God, praise Him, and minister to Him; and some of them have a special care of men.

Every Christian, and probably every other human being, has a Guardian Angel, whose duty it is to pray for him, to prompt him and help him to resist the devil, and to guard him against dangers of soul and body.

There are texts of Scripture which imply that kingdoms, churches and other communities also have Guardian Angels, and that the Archangel Michael, the Prince of the heavenly host, is the Guardian Angel of the Church at large.

21. The Earth and Man.—The last thing God made upon earth was man.

The first man was Adam; God made him of the dust of the earth.

The first woman was Eve; God formed her out of a rib of Adam.

God made them more than six thousand years ago.

He gave them the Garden of Eden, or Paradise, to dwell in,

And endowed them with grace to make them holy.

All mankind are descended from Adam and Eve.

22. The Nature of Man.—Man has two parts, a body that will die, and a soul that will never die.

The body is made of the dust of the earth.

The soul is a spirit and is created out of nothing.

It is the soul that thinks, and feels, and moves the body, and chooses to do right or wrong, to love God or not to love Him.

The soul is thus the nobler part of man.

23. God's Likeness in the Soul.—God made man to His own image and likeness.

This likeness is chiefly in our souls; for (1) our souls are spirits, and God is a spirit; (2) our souls will live for ever as God will live for ever, both being immortal; and (3) as in God there are three persons so in the soul there are three powers. These powers of the soul are memory, understanding and will.

24. Free Will.—We are able in this world either to love God, or not to love Him; we can keep His commandments or we can break them; we can be good or we can be wicked just as we choose.

But if we are good, God will reward us in heaven. If we are wicked, He will punish us in Hell.

25. Why Man was made.—God made us for His own glory.

He does not wish us to be lost in hell.

He earnestly wishes us all to be saved—that is, to go to heaven.

He wishes us therefore to save our souls by knowing Him, by loving Him, and by serving Him.

We know Him when we believe all the teaching of the Church; we love Him when we care for Him more than anyone else; and we serve Him when we keep His commandments, and practise the religion of Jesus Christ.

To know Him, to love Him and serve Him in this world, and so to come to be happy with Him for ever in heaven, is the end for which God made us.

26. The Sin of Adam.—God gave to Adam and Eve in Paradise one special commandment; he commanded them not to eat the fruit of a certain tree.

But the devil under the form of a serpent persuaded Eve to eat of it; and Eve persuaded Adam.

Thus God's commandment was broken and sin came into the world.

27. Its Punishment.—Our first parents were punished for their disobedience. They were deprived of the grace that made them holy; they lost for themselves and their descendants all right to go to heaven; they were driven out of Paradise; and they were condemned to labour, to suffer, and at length to die.

28. Original Sin.—Through the sin of Adam we were all conceived in original sin.

This sin is the guilt of Adam passed on to us.

It is called original sin because we contract it in our very origin.

29. Its Consequences.—By original sin we were deprived at our conception of sanctifying grace.

We were made unable to do any good work worthy of a reward in heaven.

And we inherited that inclination to commit actual sin which is called concupiscence.

In short, since the fall of Adam, human nature is *fallen* and *prone to evil*.

And all the descendants of Adam, with few exceptions, have offended God by actual sin.

30. Actual Sin is the sin we ourselves commit.

It is any thought, word, deed or omission against the law of God. That is, it is any breaking of God's commandments—either of those which He gave to Moses on Mount Sinai, or of those which He has given us by Christ and His Church. Or, lastly, it is the doing of anything which our conscience tells us to be wrong.

An actual sin is either mortal or venial.

31. Mortal Sin, that is, deadly or killing sin, is that which offends God grievously.

It is a sin that does great injury either to the honour of God, or to our neighbour or to ourselves.

Idolatry, murder, impurity and the like are mortal sins (see Apoc. xxi. 8).

Such sins deprive the soul of sanctifying grace, which is the supernatural life of the soul.

They are therefore called *mortal* or *deadly* sins.

It requires but one mortal sin to drive away grace from the soul and to make it an enemy of God.

For a sin to be mortal there must be :—

(1) An offence against God in a grave and important matter;

(2) A knowledge and advertence at the time it is done, that the thing is grievously wrong; and

(3) A full and perfect consent of the will to do it.

So no one can offend God mortally, unless he knows and thinks what he is doing, and yet determines to do it.

32. Venial Sin is a less grievous offence against God.

For instance, slight passions, little lies of excuse, wilful distractions in prayer and the like are venial sins.

No number of these can deprive the soul of grace, nor make it God's enemy.

They are therefore called *venial*, or *pardonable* sins, because they are more easily forgiven than mortal sins.

Yet, next to mortal sin, venial sin is the greatest evil in the world.

33. The Punishments due to Sin.—The due punishment of original sin is the loss of heaven and the deprivation of the sight of God for ever.

For actual sin we deserve to be punished with pain and torment after death.

For mortal sin we deserve to be punished for ever in the fire of hell.

For venial sin we deserve to be punished with some *temporal* punishment, or punishment *that will last for a time*, in the fire of purgatory.

And if God had not sent us a SAVIOUR, we should certainly have had to suffer these dreadful punishments.

For no prayer that we might say, no good works that we might do, could make, by themselves, satisfaction to God for the injury which is done to Him by sin.

34. The Promise of a Saviour.—On the day that Adam sinned God cursed the serpent, which was Satan.

And He said,—"I will put enmity between thee and the woman, and thy seed and her seed; she shall crush thy head, and thou shalt lie in wait for her heel" (Gen. iii. 15).

This prophecy was fulfilled after more than 4,000 years in the Blessed Virgin Mary and her Divine Son Jesus.

35. The Immaculate Conception.—There was enmity between Mary and the serpent, because she was conceived without the stain of original sin.

In other words, she was conceived in the state of grace, and was never for one moment under the power of the devil.

Mary's was therefore an Immaculate Conception.

She was thus filled with grace, and the Lord was with her, that she might be not unworthy to be the Mother of the Messias.

36. The Seed of the Woman.—Her seed or offspring was Jesus Christ our Saviour.

By giving Him birth she crushed the serpent's head.

SECOND ARTICLE OF THE CREED.

And in Jesus Christ His only Son our Lord.

37. The Divinity of Jesus Christ.—Jesus Christ is God the Son.

He was born of the Father from all eternity.

He is the Second Person of the Blessed Trinity.
He is the "Word" that was "made flesh" (John i. 14).
He is the Image of His Father's Substance.
He has the same divine nature as God the Father.
He is therefore truly God.
He is "God of God, and Light of Light."
He is equal to the Father in all things.
And He is equally with the Father, our Maker, our Master and our Lord.

THIRD ARTICLE OF THE CREED.

Who was conceived by the Holy Ghost, born of the Virgin Mary.

38. The Incarnation.—"The Word was made Flesh" (John i. 14).

This means that God the Son became man, being conceived by the power of the Holy Ghost, in the womb of the Blessed Virgin Mary.

His taking our human nature, or His being "made flesh," is called His Incarnation.

His Incarnation took place nearly 1900 years ago.

39. The Birth of our Redeemer.—Our Lord Jesus Christ was born of the Virgin Mary.

The Blessed Virgin is therefore His mother.

And because He is Lord and God (see John xx. 28) his Mother was rightly addressed by St. Elizabeth as "the Mother of my Lord" (Luke i. 43), and is rightly called by the Church "the Mother of God."

Our Lord Jesus Christ had no man for His Father.

St. Joseph, the husband of Mary, was His guardian or foster-father.

Our Lord was born upon Christmas Day, in a stable in the city of Bethlehem, in Palestine or the Holy Land.

40. The Humanity of Jesus Christ.—Our Lord Jesus Christ has had since the moment of His Incarnation a body and soul like ours.

He is therefore a real man.

41. The Hypostatic Union.—Jesus Christ has now two natures: He is God, and He is Man.

The nature of God He has had from all eternity.

The nature of man He took at His Incarnation.

Yet He is only one person.

For in the one person of Jesus Christ the nature of God and the nature of man are joined together; and their union in Him is called the Hypostatic (or personal) Union.

42. Its Consequences.—(1) Because Christ was truly God and truly Man, it is true to say of Him:—

That He was born of the Father, and that He was born of Mary:

That He is the Son of God, and that He is the Son of Man.

That He is the Immortal—Who lives for ever and ever,—and yet that He died:

That as God He is equal to the Father, but that as Man He is less than the Father.

For whatever is true of God is true of Christ, and whatever is true of human nature, except sin, is also true of Christ.

(2) It is also clear from the fact of His being both God and Man:—

That whatever He did was the work of God:

That in Christ God spoke and suffered and died:

And that all His actions were Divine, infinitely holy and infinitely meritorious.

43. Events of His Life.—On the very night of His birth He was visited by shepherds; on the eighth day He was circumcised; on the fortieth day He was presented in the temple to the Lord; some time after He was visited and adored by wise men from the East; and was taken by Mary and Joseph into Egypt, to prevent His being slain by King Herod. At twelve years old He was brought to Jerusalem to the feast of the Passover or Pasch, when He was lost by His parents, and found after three days in the temple among the doctors of the law: after which He returned with His parents to Nazareth, and was subject to them.

When thirty years old or thereabouts, He was baptised by St. John the Baptist. He was led into the desert, fasted forty days and forty nights, and was tempted three times by Satan. Some days after, St. John confessed Him publicly, saying, "Behold the Lamb of God." The next three years He spent in preaching, teaching and working miracles.

44. His Miracles.—He worked His first miracle at a marriage feast at Cana in Galilee, where He changed water into wine (John ii. 1—11).

This miracle He worked at His Mother's request, though He said that His hour was not yet come.

Thus He showed us how much He loved His Mother, and how surely He would answer her prayers.

He afterwards wrought many other miracles.

He fed at one time five thousand men with five barley loaves and two fishes, and at another four thousand men with seven loaves and a few little fishes.

He calmed the stormy sea, saying "Peace, be still."

He cured all kinds of diseases.

He cast out devils from people that were possessed by them.

And three times it is recorded that He raised the dead to life.

By working these miracles He showed that He was the Son of God.

45. His Teaching.—He taught both by word and example the practice of all virtues.

He gave out afresh the ten commandments of the law.

He explained them so as to teach the perfect life.

He changed the Covenant of Fear into the Covenant of Love.

He gave a new commandment to all men, which was, that they should love one another as He had loved them.

He laid down the golden rule of conduct—"Whatsoever you would that men should do unto you, do you also unto them" (Matt. vii. 12).

And He taught that we must forgive one another from our hearts.

Moreover He taught His disciples how to pray, and assured them that whatever they asked in His name they should receive.

He instituted the seven Sacraments.

He called and instructed the twelve Apostles.

And on Peter their chief He founded the Catholic Church, which was to teach in His name for ever.

FOURTH ARTICLE OF THE CREED.

Suffered under Pontius Pilate, was crucified, dead and buried.

46. The Passion and death of Christ.—The chief sufferings of Christ were these:—

(1) He grieved for our sins with such anguish that He fell into an agony and sweat of blood in the garden of Gethsemani.

(2) By order of Pontius Pilate, the Roman governor over the Jews, He was bound to a pillar and scourged, or beaten with whips and rods.

(3) He was crowned in mockery with a wreath or crown of sharp thorns.

(4) He was made to carry His cross to Calvary.

(5) On Calvary He was nailed to the Cross, and after great pain He died upon it.

These sufferings are called His *Passion*.

47. Why He suffered.—The chief men among the Jews became His enemies. They hated Him for His goodness, and they envied His popularity. At length they determined to kill Him, and His hour being come, He gave Himself into their hands.

Thus He suffered of His own free will.

He suffered that we might be forgiven.

He suffered for all, even for those that crucified Him.

He suffered as Man, (1) because as God He could not suffer, and (2) because He suffered for the sins of men.

But still He that suffered was God.

48. The Worth of His Death.—His death was an act of obedience to His Father's will.

As the act of a Divine Person it gave more glory to God the Father than all the sins of men could take away.

And therefore it could atone, or make satisfaction for the sins of the whole world.

Our Blessed Lord's death is called the Sacrifice of the Cross.

49. Sacrifice is an act of worship that can lawfully be paid to God alone.

It is offered by slaying, or changing, or making away with something, in order to signify that God is our Master, and can do with us as we do with the thing destroyed.

The thing which in this way is offered to God is called the victim.

It must be offered by a minister, called a priest, whom God has appointed to offer it.

There have been a priesthood and sacrifices from the beginning of the world.

50. The Sacrifices of the Old Law.—These were of four kinds:—

(1) The Holocausts, or whole-burnt offerings made solely to acknowledge that God is the Lord and Master of man, and of all man calls his own.

(2) Thank-offerings, made likewise to thank Him for His benefits to man.

(3) Sin-offerings made especially to beg mercy and pardon for sin.

(4) Peace-offerings, to implore fresh graces and blessings.

51. The Sacrifice of the Cross.—Our Blessed Lord's death was at once a Holocaust, a Thank-offering, a Sin-offering and a Peace-offering.

Our Lord Jesus Christ Himself was the priest that offered it; and our Lord Jesus Christ Himself was the victim. For He offered His body to death, and His soul to suffering.

52. What He merited by it.—He merited *for Himself* His resurrection, the glory of His name, and the adoration of the universe.

He merited *for us* justification, eternal life, and all other gifts of grace.

53. His Burial.—When Jesus was dead His body was taken down from the Cross and laid in a new sepulchre or tomb.

It was there embalmed by Nicodemus.

A great stone was rolled to the door of the tomb; and the Pharisees set a guard around it, lest His disciples might steal Him away, and say that He had risen from the dead.

He died and was buried on Good Friday.

FIFTH ARTICLE OF THE CREED.

He descended into hell; the third day He rose again from the dead.

54. His Descent into Hell.—When Jesus died His soul went down into that part of hell, called limbo.

The word limbo means border-land. It was the abode of those that had died before Christ in a state of grace, and were waiting to enter heaven.

55. His Resurrection.—On Easter Sunday, early in the morning, our Saviour rose from the dead.

His soul came back to His body, and His body lived once more.

An angel rolled back the stone and terrified the guards; and Jesus came forth glorified and impassible.

56. His Appearances.—After His resurrection, it is recorded that He appeared to His disciples eleven times during forty days. He appeared to Mary Magdalene; to the other holy women; to Cephas (that is, Peter the Apostle); to the two disciples going to Emmaus; to the disciples in Jerusalem, where he instituted the sacrament of penance; to the disciples with St. Thomas, eight days after His resurrection; to the disciples at the Sea of Tiberias, when He charged St. Peter to feed His lambs and sheep (John xxi. 17); to the eleven on the mount in Galilee, when He charged them to "teach all nations" (Matt. xxviii. 19); to above five hundred brethren at once; to St. James; and lastly, to all the Apostles, when He told them to tarry in Jerusalem for the coming of the Holy Ghost. He spoke at these appearances about the Kingdom of God (Acts i. 3).

SIXTH ARTICLE OF THE CREED.

He ascended into heaven, sitteth at the right hand of God the Father Almighty.

57. The Ascension.—On the fortieth day after His resurrection He led His disciples to Bethany and blessed them and ascended from Mount Olivet into heaven.

He then entered heaven as man. As God He had always been there.

He went up to heaven as man—(1) to be rewarded in the body for the work which He had done in the body; (2) to be our Advocate, *i.e.*, to plead for us by His Passion; (3) to prepare a place for His faithful followers; and (4) to send down the Holy Ghost.

58. His Place in Heaven.—He sitteth as man on the right hand of God the Father.

His human nature, which is a created thing, is of course less than His divine nature, which is uncreated.

But these two natures have been united at the Incarnation, and can never more be separated;

And therefore Christ, even as man, is in the glory of God the Father, in the highest place in heaven, at the right hand of God.

59. The Worship due to Him.—He must be worshipped with the profoundest adoration, for He is God.

And this adoration is due to every part of His sacred humanity.

For His Body is God's Body, His Soul is God's Soul, His Blood is God's Blood, and His Heart is God's Heart.

So we worship His Body and Soul, His Precious Blood, His Sacred Heart, and His Wounded Hands, and Feet, and Side, (1) because they are united to the person of God the Son; and (2) because by them He has redeemed us from sin, saved us from hell, given us blessings without number, and thereby merited our everlasting gratitude.

60. His Names.—As God made man, His first and greatest name is JESUS, or *Saviour*. His second name is CHRIST, the *Anointed*, or the *Consecrated* One.

He is consecrated Prophet, Priest, and King: Prophet, because He was the Great Teacher; Priest, because He offered Himself once in sacrifice upon the Cross, and daily renews that sacrifice in the Holy Mass; and King, because He is Founder, Head, and Ruler of the Church which is the kingdom of God.

61. Christ the One Mediator.—He is called the "One Mediator of God and man." (1 Tim. ii. 5).

An angel that brings a message from God to man may be called a mediator between God and man; or a saint, like Moses, that intercedes with God for sinners, may also be called a mediator.

Our Blessed Lord was the great Mediator in both these ways.

But further, He alone actually endured the punishment that was due to our sins; He alone paid the debt that was owing by us; He alone made a real and complete satisfaction for our misdeeds.

And further, He alone united in Himself the nature of God and the nature of man.

In these two latter ways He is the one and only mediator between God and man. And all other mediation can avail only by its resting in the first place on His.

SEVENTH ARTICLE OF THE CREED.

From thence He shall come to judge the living and the dead.

62. The Second Coming of Christ.—Our Lord will come again openly at the end of the world, to judge the living and the dead.

The good He will reward in heaven; the wicked He will punish in hell.

The day of his coming is called the Last Day, or the Day of Judgment.

EIGHTH ARTICLE OF THE CREED.

I believe in the Holy Ghost.

63. The Holy Ghost is the Third Person of the Blessed Trinity.

He is the uncreated love of the Father and the Son.

He proceeds or comes forth from the Father and the Son.

He is equal to Them, and is the same Lord and God as They are.

64. Pentecost.—On Whit Sunday, or the day of Pentecost, that is, fifty days after our Lord's resurrection, and ten days after his ascension, the Holy Ghost came down from heaven upon the Apostles.

A sound was heard, as of a mighty wind, in the house where they were sitting;

There appeared tongues of fire, or a lambent flame, sitting upon each of them;

And they were all filled with the Holy Ghost, and with power and grace to enable them to preach the Gospel and to plant the Church.

The Holy Ghost was thus sent into the world, by God the Father and God the Son.

And His coming was due to the merits of Christ.

65. The twofold Office of the Holy Ghost. —As Creation is more especially the work of God the Father, and Redemption the work of God the Son, so Illumination and Sanctification are especially the work of God the Holy Ghost.

He is the Spirit of Truth, and the Giver of Life, that is, of Grace.

Or, in other words, He is God the Enlightener, and God the Sanctifier.

As the Enlightener He works chiefly in the Church at large.

As the Sanctifier He works chiefly in the souls of men, one by one.

66. His Work in the Church.—The Holy Ghost united the disciples into one body, the mystical body of Christ, and thus became the Soul of the Christian Church.

He has dwelt in the Church ever since, and will abide with it for ever (John xiv. 16).

And therefore He makes it one, because He is one.

He makes it holy because He is the fount of holiness.

He makes it imperishable because He is everlasting.

And He makes it infallible, because He guides, enlightens, teaches, and sanctifies it, without intermission.

67. His Work in the Soul.—He prompts and helps the soul to do good works by actual grace.

He makes the soul righteous and holy, that is, He justifies and sanctifies it by habitual grace,

And He bestows upon the justified soul, according as it makes good use of His grace, the three virtues of Faith, Hope and Charity, His Seven Gifts, His Twelve Fruits, the Eight Beatitudes, and various Sacramental Graces.

NINTH ARTICLE OF THE CREED.

The Holy Catholic Church, the Communion of Saints.

68. The Catholic Church is the union or society of the followers of Jesus Christ.

It was founded by our Blessed Lord Himself.

It is called in Scripture the Kingdom of Heaven, or the Kingdom of God.

The Church is made up of two classes—the pastors and their flocks; or the clergy whose duty it is to teach, and the laity who hear and practise, but have no authority publicly to teach, the word of God.

69. The Teaching Church.—Our Lord chose twelve of his disciples, whom He called His Apostles, to be chief preachers, and teachers and rulers of the rest.

He first instructed them in the mysteries of the kingdom of heaven (Matt. xiii. 11), and in all that He had heard from the Father (Jo. xv. 15).

He promised them the Holy Ghost for their own perpetual teacher and guide (John xiv. 16, xiv. 26, xvi. 13).

And He commanded them to preach the Gospel to every creature (Mark xvi. 15).

Thus He founded His Church by calling His Apostles and by giving them power to make other disciples.

First therefore the Apostles, and secondly the bishops their successors, (with the other clergy for delegates and assistants), constitute the teaching Church.

70. The Primacy of St. Peter.—That the Church might be one, as Christ and the Father are One (see John xvii. 21), our Blessed Lord appointed St. Peter to be the First in dignity and the Chief in authority of all the Apostles, and, therefore, the Centre of Unity for all the Church.

This Primacy was promised to St. Peter when our Lord changed his name, or declared that it should be changed, from Simon into Cephas or Peter (John i. 42); and still more clearly, some time after, when He said to him, "Thou art Peter *(a Rock)* and upon this Rock I will build my Church, and the gates of hell shall not prevail against it. And I will give to thee the keys of the kingdom of heaven. And whatsoever thou shalt bind upon earth, it shall be bound also in heaven; and whatsoever thou shalt loose upon earth, it shall be loosed also in heaven" (Matt. xvi. 18-19).

And lastly, on the night of His betrayal, He said to St. Peter, "Satan hath desired to have you (ὑμᾶς) that he may sift you as wheat; but I have prayed for *thee* (σοῦ) that thy faith fail not; and thou being once converted, confirm *thy* brethren" (Luke xxii., 31, 32).

Here notice (1) that Christ gave Peter His own proper name and designation, for Christ is the "Rock" (1 Cor. x. 4), the "Living Stone" and "Chief Cornerstone" (1 Pet. ii. 4, 6); (2) that He who has "the *keys* of death and hell" and "the *key* of David" finally to open and finally to shut (Apoc. i. 18 and iii. 7), gave "the keys of the kingdom of heaven to Peter; (3) that he promised, first, and singly, and personally to Peter the power of binding and loosing, promised afterwards to the others (Matt. xviii. 18); and (4) that all were to be in danger, but Peter's faith alone was to be unfailing, *in order* that he might confirm the rest.

These promises were fulfilled and the primacy finally conferred upon Peter when, after the resurrection, Christ said to him, "Feed My lambs; feed (rule) My sheep" (John xxi. 15, 17; ποιμαίνειν is more than βόσκειν; it suggests—"Be the kingly shepherd of My sheep," for Christ had called Himself ὁ ποιμήν, the Shepherd.

71. St. Peter as Primate.—Accordingly, St. Peter is always first in the lists of the Apostles, and his name appears oftener than that of any other. In the list in the Acts his name again is first. He takes the lead in the choosing of Matthias. He is the first to preach, and defends the other disciples. He is the first to work a miracle. He is spokesman for himself and John, when they are apprehended. It is Peter who reprimands Ananias and Saphira; Peter's shadow that heals the sick; Peter who speaks for the rest before the high priest. He is the first to receive the Gentiles. For him alone when imprisoned is "prayer made without ceasing by the Church," and he is miraculously delivered. And when Paul and Barnabas had to appeal against the Judaisers to the Apostles and Priests at Jerusalem, St. Peter delivers the first infallible judgment of the Church, to which James and the rest at once assent (Acts xv.).

72. St. Peter Bishop of Rome.—St. Peter was Bishop first of Antioch; but finally he fixed his see, that is, the seat of his bishopric, at Rome. He was Bishop of Rome for twenty-five years; and at length suffered martyrdom, together with St. Paul, in the year 67.

Of these facts there is clear and decisive evidence in the ancient Christian writers. The "Babylon" from which St. Peter wrote (1 Peter v. 13) is held by them all, and by all moderns, too, except a few Protestants, to have been the city of Rome.

73. The Primacy Perpetual.—It has always been a Catholic tradition and doctrine, asserted and believed from the earliest times, that the Bishop of Rome succeeds by right divine to St. Peter's Primacy, and is, like him, the Vicar of Christ, and Head, on earth, of the Universal Church.

The Bishop of Rome is therefore called the *Pope*, that is, the *Father*, because he is the spiritual Father of all true followers of Christ.

74. The Nature and Effects of the Primacy.—Full power, as we have seen, was given to the Pope, in Blessed Peter, by our Lord Jesus Christ, to rule, to nourish, and to govern the Church.

Bishops, priests, and laity, therefore, are subject to the Pope in all that regards faith and morals, discipline and Church government.

And the effects of their submission are that the Church is one flock, obeying one shepherd; that the "faith once delivered to the saints" has been preserved entire and uncorrupted; that Catholics have a simple test of orthodoxy, communion with Rome; that through their acknowledgment of the Pope's supremacy millions of Catholics are absolutely at one in faith, and in the essential practices of religion; and that all these millions whom Christ has thus made one, are witnesses of His wisdom and power and Divinity (see John xvii. 21) Who has made His kingdom such a marvel of supernatural unity.

Whereas those who refuse to submit to the Pope are divided into hundreds of warring sects, each in hopeless confusion and uncertainty.

75. The Pope's Infallibility.—When the Pope, as Shepherd and Teacher of all Christians, by virtue of his Supreme Apostolic Authority, defines a doctrine regarding faith or morals to be held by the whole Church,—then the Pope is infallible.

That is to say, in cases of doubt or dispute, whether any doctrine is or is not contained in the Christian Revelation, or is or is not in accordance with it, or whether any act is in itself morally right or wrong, the Pope is the highest judge on earth, the final and infallible court of appeal.

By virtue of his Primacy, his solemn decision in all such cases is binding upon the consciences of all the faithful.

And therefore, there is involved in the fact of his Primacy a Divine guarantee that his final and solemn decision, in matters of faith and morals, shall be always right and true.

But observe, the Pope has no power to make new doctrine. Infallibility is not inspiration. New truths are not revealed to the Pope as they were to the Apostles. His office is only to maintain and expound the ancient "faith once delivered to the saints" (Jude i. 3).

76. The Marks or Notes of the Church.—
The marks of the Church are Oneness, Holiness, Catholicity, and Apostolicity. They are properties or endowments, which the true Church of Christ must needs possess.

77. Oneness or Unity.—The Church is One, (1) because it is the only Church which Christ established, and (2) because it is united in itself.

All Catholics have one head upon earth who is the Pope, and one Lord in heaven who is Jesus Christ.

All Catholics have one and the same faith.

They have all the same sacraments.

And they all worship God, by one and the same sacrifice, the sacrifice of the Mass.

78. Holiness.—The Church is Holy in its Head, in its Soul, in its doctrines, in its sacraments, and in its Saints.

Its Head is Jesus Christ, who is infinitely holy because He is God.

Its Soul is the Holy Ghost, and He too is holy because He is God.

Its doctrines are holy, because they have been taught by Jesus Christ.

Its sacraments are holy, because they are the chief means by which Christ's merits are applied to our souls.

And Christ our Lord has sanctified by means of His Church, with its doctrines and sacraments, many millions of people.

79. Catholicity.—The Church of Christ is Catholic or Universal in doctrine, time, and place.

It is Catholic in doctrine because it teaches the whole counsel of God (Acts xx. 27), or all the truth as it is in Jesus (Eph. iv. 21).

It is Catholic in time, because it has taught this truth in every age since the time of Christ, and will teach the same until the end of the world.

It is Catholic in place because it was intended by Christ to be the Church of all nations, and the one Ark of Salvation for all, and because it has actually made disciples in every country of the world.

80. Apostolicity.—The Church is Apostolic because it was founded by Christ in his twelve Apostles; and because its bishops have been consecrated one by another in unbroken succession from them. This is called the Apostolic Succession.

And through the Apostles it has from Christ, its doctrine, its orders, and its mission.

Its doctrine is what it teaches.

Its orders are its bishops, priests, deacons and other ministers who receive their powers chiefly through the sacrament of Holy Order.

And its mission is the authority whereby its ministers validly and lawfully do that which they are sent to do, namely, preach the Gospel and administer the sacraments.

81. The Use of the Four Marks.—Unity, Holiness, Catholicity, and Apostolicity are clearly properties which the true Church of Christ must possess.

Now the Roman Church does manifestly possess them;

And all other churches as manifestly do not possess them;

And therefore they are marks of genuineness, or proofs that the Church of Rome is the Church of God.

82. Other Properties of the Church.—Besides the four manifest properties of the Church which are called its Marks or Notes, the Church has other properties which spring from the in-dwelling presence of the Holy Ghost.

The Church is indefectible or imperishable, visible, infallible, and necessary for all.

83. Indefectibility.—The Church can neither fail nor change.

Its practices of devotion and its discipline, or temporary laws, may vary, but its doctrine and its mission are unchangeable.

84. Visibility.—The church is likened to a city set upon a hill (Matt. v. 14).

It is a society, a polity, a kingdom. It is therefore visible to the whole world.

85. Infallibility.—The voice of the Church is the voice of Christ; for it speaks with His authority.

For He said to the Pastors of the Church,—"I am with you all days;" and "He that heareth you heareth Me," and, "As the Father hath sent Me, I also send you" (Matt. xxviii. 20. Luke x. 16. John xx. 21).

And the "Spirit of Truth," He said, "shall abide with you and shall be in you" (John xiv. 17).

"He will teach you all things and bring all things to your mind whatsoever I shall have said to you" (xiv. 26).

St. Paul called the Church the "pillar and ground of truth" (1 Tim. iii. 15).

And hence in faith and morals the Church is our infallible guide.

What its bishops all teach and its people believe is infallibly true.

86. Necessity.—The Church is the one channel of truth and grace, established by Jesus Christ.

It is charged to teach all nations (Matt. xxviii. 19). All nations are therefore bound to hear it.

"Whoever believes will be saved; whoever believes not will be condemned" (Mark xvi. 16).

So that all men are bound by a Divine command to become by baptism members of the Church, out of which there is therefore no salvation.

87. The Completion of Revelation.—The Holy Ghost is the Spirit of Truth.

As the Spirit of Truth, He reminded the Apostles of all that Christ had taught, He enlightened them to understand it, and he revealed new truths to their intelligence.

He taught them, not by words, but by spiritual illumination.

He thus completed the Christian Revelation; so that since the time of the Apostles no new revelation has ever been given as a part of Catholic Faith, nor has any ever been needed.

88. Divine Tradition.—The Holy Ghost has preserved all the truths of revelation in the collective mind of the Church.

He has enabled the Church (1) to pass these truths on without change from generation to generation; (2) to understand them more fully and more clearly in course of time; and (3) to express them more and more plainly in words.

The handing down of revealed truths from age to age is called *Tradition*.

And the progress of the Church in the knowledge and in the expression in words of revealed truths is called the *Development of Christian Doctrine.*

89. The Preservation of Revealed Truth; the Instruments of Tradition.—Divine Truth has come down to us chiefly in the following ways :—

(1) In the Seven Sacraments.
(2) In the Apostles' Creed and the Decalogue.
(3) In the New Testament, or Christian Scripture.
(4) In the later Creeds of the Church.
(5) In the decrees of the Œcumenical Councils.
(6) In the definitions of the Sovereign Pontiffs.
(7) In the writings of the Saints, Fathers, Doctors, Historians and Theologians of the Church.

90. The Seven Sacraments.—The truths of the Gospel were enshrined (as it were) by Christ Himself in the Seven Sacraments.

Thus, Baptism implied the doctrines of creation, the fall of Adam, original and actual sin, and the new birth of grace.

Confirmation involved a belief in the Holy Ghost with a knowledge of His gifts and graces.

Penance and Extreme Unction spoke the need of repentance, the virtue of contrition, the cleansing power of the precious blood, the forgiveness of post-baptismal sin, and the absolving power of the priesthood.

Holy Order expressed the authority and endowments of the Church's hierarchy.

Matrimony, as a Christian sacrament, was an indissoluble union from the beginning, and a symbol of the loving and everlasting union between Christ and the Church (Eph. v. 23—33).

And the Holy Eucharist was a sacrament and sacrifice in which almost every Christian truth was implied. In it and its liturgy were reflected the doctrines of the incarnation, the redemption, the union of Christ with his Church, the communion of saints, purgatory, the obligation and efficacy of prayer, and many others.

And every sacrament supposed in the recipient of it a belief in the divinity of Jesus Christ, and some knowledge of His life and teaching.

91. The Creed and the Decalogue.—The Apostles, before dispersing, are said to have composed that short profession of faith which is called the Apostles' Creed.

The Apostles' Creed is a summary of the Gospel truth, as the Ten Commandments are a summary of the moral law.

All the truths and all the laws of the Christian religion, are contained or implied in these two summaries.

In the Creed, the Commandments, and the sacramental rites, the faith has been preserved and propagated from the day of Pentecost until now.

92. The Christian Scripture.—After the Christian religion had been preached in many countries by the Apostles and their disciples, its doctrines, laws, and practices were in great part written in the books of the New Testament.

These books are — The Gospels of SS. Matthew, Mark, Luke and John; the Acts of the Apostles, written by St Luke; fourteen Epistles of St. Paul, one of St. James, two of St. Peter, three of St. John, one of St. Jude; and the Apocalypse or Revelations of St. John the Apostle.

These books, like those of the Old Testament, were all inspired by the Holy Ghost. That is, God is their principal Author. He prompted their human authors to write them. He suggested to their minds what truths they were to write; and He preserved them from all error in what they wrote.

93. The Utility of the New Testament.— The New Testament contains (1) reasons for believing in Jesus Christ, (2) reasons for believing in the Catholic Church, and (3) examples of our Lord's and the Apostles' teaching.

(1) The Gospels record the miracles of Jesus Christ.

They record His prophecies and their fulfilment.

They record instances of His knowledge of men's thoughts, and of hidden events.

They remark His fulfilment of Old Testament prophecies.

They record the testimony borne to Him by angels.

They record His own 'claims to be God, and the witnessing words of God the Father to His Divinity.

They declare His resurrection from the dead, His subsequent appearances to His disciples, and His glorious ascension into heaven.

Moreover, they describe His character; they show forth His love and obedience to His Father, His firmness of purpose, His meekness, humility and purity, His charity and never-failing kindness, His forgiveness of injuries, and His pity for sinners side by side with His hatred of sin—in all, such a character as can belong to the Son of God alone. These things are proofs that Christ is God.

(2) The New Testament bears witness to the Church. It points to the Church as a living and infallible guide.

In the Gospels we read of its foundation; of the calling of its first pastors; of the promises Christ made to them; and of the charge which he gave them to teach all nations.

In the Acts of the Apostles we see the Church fulfilling its mission.

And in the Epistles its pastors are described as being sent by God, as having the Spirit to know the things of God, as having the mind of Christ, as being God's coadjutors, ministers of Christ, and dispensers of the mysteries of God, and as having to render an account for the souls of the people.

(3) The New Testament records examples of the teaching of Christ and of His Apostles.

The gist of some of our Lord's discourses, and sometimes His very words are preserved in the Gospels.

The preaching of the Apostles is sketched in the book of the Acts.

And the Epistles contain treasures of supplementary teaching.

94. The Insufficiency of Scripture as a Rule of Faith.—But the New Testament contains no complete statement of Christian faith and practices.

It contains no particular directions on the subject of public worship.

It gives in full no rite for the administration of any sacrament.

It pre-supposes in its readers a knowledge of all such things.

Moreover, it nowhere tells us what books are inspired by God, nor even how many such books there are, nor how to distinguish them from spurious imitations.

The knowledge of these things has been preserved by tradition, that is, in the memory of the Catholic Church.

Yet the knowledge of these things is necessary for the very existence of the Christian religion.

And therefore "the Bible, and the Bible only" can never be the religion of real Christians, for Christianity is the Bible and very much more.

95. The Interpretation of Scripture.—In Scripture "there are some things hard to be understood" (2 Peter iii. 16).

Scripture "without note or comment" is therefore dangerous.

The ignorant or unstable may wrest it to their own destruction (2 Peter iii. 16).

Some comment or explanation is therefore needed.

And God has given us a comment or explanation of his own.

This comment is the Church's traditional teaching.

For the same Holy Ghost who enlightened the Apostles to write, has enlightened the Church to understand.

In reading Scripture, therefore, we must remember—

(1) That the Church's interpretation of any text, whether contained in a definition of Pope or Council, or known by the unanimous consent of the Fathers, is infallibly the true one.

(2) That an interpretation which contradicts this, or which contradicts any article of faith, is certainly erroneous.

For Scripture is the word of God, only in the sense in which it was written.

And the Church alone is infallible in its knowledge of that sense.

96. The Later Creeds of the Church.—

These are:—

(1) The Nicene Creed, composed at the Council of Nice in the year 325, and enlarged at Constantinople in 381.

It contains a more explicit profession of faith in God the Son and God the Holy Ghost.

It was directed against the Arians, who denied that Christ was God, and against other heretics who denied that the Holy Ghost was God.

(2) The Athanasian Creed, composed in the fifth century.

It clearly asserts the doctrines of the Blessed Trinity, and of the Incarnation.

It is called after St. Athanasius, because, just before it was composed, he had bravely defended those doctrines.

(3) The Creed of Pope Pius IV, composed after the Council of Trent.

It asserts, in plain words, the principal doctrines denied by Protestants.

97. Other Instruments of Tradition.—

These are:—

(1) The decrees of the general councils.

A general council is an assembly to which all the bishops of the Catholic world are summoned by the Pope, and which is presided over by him or his legates. The decrees of a council touching faith or morals, when confirmed by the Pope, are infallible.

(2) The dogmatic decisions of the Sovereign Pontiffs. These, too, are infallible, because in making them, the Pope is acting as Shepherd and Teacher of the whole Church.

(3) The writings of the Saints, Doctors, Fathers, Theologians, and Historians of the Church. These are the witnesses in every age of the Church's doctrine. What they all, or nearly all, hand down as doctrines of the Church, though they be found neither in Scripture, nor in any definition of Pope or Council, are certainly true, and of apostolical authority.

On such testimony we believe, for instance, that the Mother of God was all her life a virgin; that she was assumed both body and soul into heaven; and that all baptised Christians have Guardian Angels.

98. The Members of the Church.

—All Catholics, both those in the state of grace, and those in mortal sin, are members of the Church.

All other baptised people, who are not separated from the Church by their own wilful heresy or schism, or by apostasy, or by excommunication, are also members of the Church, though they may not know it.

And even the dead, if they died in the Lord, that is, in the state of grace, are still members of the Church.

Thus, the members of the Church are, some on earth, some in purgatory, and some in heaven.

The Church on earth is the Church Militant; the Church in purgatory is the Church Suffering; and the Church in heaven is the Church Triumphant.

99. The Church Militant.

— Man's life on earth is a warfare.

On our way towards heaven we have enemies to fight. These enemies are the devil, the world, and the flesh.

The devil is Satan with all his wicked angels, who tempt us to sin.

The world is the company of those that love vanity, godless knowledge, unchristian education, riches, pleasure or sin better than God and religion.

The flesh is our own passions and bad inclinations, which are the effects of original sin.

And the Church Militant is, in effect, the company of those who avoid evil and do good, and thus combat the devil, the world, and the flesh.

100. The Church Suffering.—The Church Suffering means the souls in purgatory.

There is a purgatory or a place of cleansing (1) for those that depart this life in venial sin; and (2) for those that have sinned and been forgiven, but have not suffered in their lifetime, nor had remitted all the temporal punishment that was due to their sins.

Such souls are in the state of grace, and therefore, they cannot be punished in hell.

But neither can they enter heaven, for nothing defiled can enter there (Apoc. xxi. 27).

And therefore they are sent for a time to a place of punishment and purification, which we call purgatory.

There they suffer a two-fold punishment:

They are deprived for a time of the sight of God, for which they long,

And they suffer besides, in proportion to their imperfections, some lesser torment, being "saved yet so as by fire" (1 Cor. iii. 15).

When fully cleansed they enter heaven.

101. The Church Triumphant.—The Church Triumphant is the Church in heaven.

It is composed of the souls of the saints.

These are they that have fought the good fight, that have conquered the devil, the world and the flesh, that died in grace, and are now in possession of their reward.

They are all supremely happy.

They are the well-tried servants and special friends of God.

They know Him and see Him as He is (1 John iii. 2), in His magnificence and beauty.

And they love Him with unspeakable love.

They have the angels for their companions.

They have great knowledge, both of the mysteries of faith, and of created things.

They know much, if not all, that happens upon earth.

They are freed from all evil, from all danger of sinning, and from every kind of sorrow.

And besides that glory which is common to all, each saint in heaven has a special glory of his own, as the reward of his own good deeds.

This special glory is called his crown.

For the description of heaven see Apoc. vii, xxi, xxii.

102. The Communion of Saints. — The saints in heaven, the souls in purgatory, and the members of the Church Militant, who are called to be saints (Rom. i. 7), all form one Church.

They have all the same Father, who is God.

They have all the same Saviour and Lord, who is Jesus Christ.

They are therefore all brethren, and members of one family.

They love each other for God their Father's sake.

And they benefit each other by means of prayer and good works.

This relationship between the children of God is the Communion of Saints.

We have therefore a communion, (1) with each other upon earth; (2) with the souls in purgatory; and (3) with the saints in heaven.

103. Our Communion with Each Other. — We have all the same faith,

We have all the same hope.
We have all the same bond of charity.
We have all the same sacraments and sacrifice.
And we have all one head upon earth, who is the Pope.
That is, we have one and the same religion, the whole world over,
And we worship God as so many members in one great body.
Our Masses, prayers, and other good works, are offered in part for all our brethren,
And they draw down blessings from God, not only upon those who offer them, but also upon the Church at large.

104. Our Communion with the Souls in Purgatory.—As long as we are in the body we can make satisfaction for our sins.

But the poor souls in purgatory can do nothing but suffer.

They can offer no prayers or other good works instead of their allotted punishment.

But we, who are still upon earth, can pray, offer Mass, give alms, do penance, gain indulgences, for their benefit.

And in view of these works of ours, when done in grace, God shortens their punishment.

For the Scripture says, "It is a holy and wholesome thought to pray for the dead that they may be loosed from sins" (2 Macch. xii. 46).

105. Our Communion with the Saints in Heaven.—The blessed Virgin Mary, the holy Angels, the Apostles, Martyrs and other Saints in Heaven are the faithful servants and special friends of God.

And therefore we honour and worship them.

Especially do we honour and worship the Blessed Virgin Mary.

She is the best and purest of all God's creatures.

She was chosen of all women to be the Mother of His Son.

She is now the Queen of Heaven, the most beloved of God, and the nearest to His throne.

Most lovingly therefore do we worship Mary, whom our God has delighted so to honour.

We worship the Blessed Virgin and the Saints, by keeping their festivals, by commemorating them in the Mass, by saying and singing their praises, and by honouring their relics and images.

Moreover, we ask both the Saints and Angels to pray for us.

And God grants us through their prayers many graces and blessings.

TENTH ARTICLE OF THE CREED.

The Forgiveness of Sins.

106. The Meaning of this Article.—This article means that God has left to the pastors of His Church, chiefly in the sacraments of baptism and penance, the power of remitting sin, both original and actual.

That such is the meaning of this article is clear from its very position.

For on the Protestant view of forgiveness, or of justification by faith alone, "The Forgiveness of Sins" should have been the *fifth* or *sixth* article of the Creed.

But being, as it is, the *tenth* article—coming *after* "The Holy Ghost; the Holy Catholic Church; the Communion of Saints,"—it suggests the true Catholic and scriptural doctrine, namely, that the forgiveness of sins has been merited by the Death of Christ, is effected by the Holy Ghost, and is to be obtained *through the instrumentality of the Church.*

In other words, the position of this article gives it a sacramental meaning.

107. Original Sin is that sin, or rather guilt, in which, owing to the sin of Adam, every human creature is conceived.

This sin, though far less displeasing to God than any mortal sin of our own committing, is nevertheless a real mortal or deadly sin, both in its nature and in its effects.

For it deprives all human beings at the very moment of their origin of the in-dwelling presence of the Holy Ghost.

It deprives them of sanctifying grace or righteousness.

It deprives them of all right to enter heaven.

And it makes them children of wrath, deserving of eternal exclusion from the sight of God.

108. Actual Sin is every sin which we ourselves commit. It is either mortal or venial.

A venial sin is one that bedims the lustre of a holy soul, and offends God, but does not deprive the soul of grace, nor excite God's eternal wrath, nor merit eternal punishment.

A mortal sin, on the other hand, is a grievous offence against God.

By committing a mortal sin, we strike against God's Majesty; we injure His loving kindness; we trample on His law.

By mortal sin, therefore, we drive God from our souls; we make Him hate us; we waste the sacred blood of Christ; we crucify Christ again to ourselves, "making Him a mockery" (Heb. vi. 6).

By mortal sin, therefore, we really merit eternal punishment. Any punishment less than the eternal fire of hell would not be a just and fitting punishment for one mortal sin knowingly and wilfully committed.

Holy Scripture is full of this truth. See especially 1 Cor. vi. 9; Gal. v. 21; Isaiah xxxiv. 10; Matt. xxv. 41; Apoc. xxi. 8.

109. God the Forgiver.—Bad as sin is, God is always ready to forgive the repenting sinner.

"As I live, saith the Lord God, I desire not the death of the wicked, but that the wicked turn from his way, and live" (Ezech. xxxiii. 11).

And therefore God sent His Son Jesus Christ to bear our sorrows, and to suffer death once for all upon the Cross, to save us from hell, which is the "second death" (Apoc. xxi. 8).

Hence all the labours, sufferings, fastings, prayers of Christ, all for the conversion of sinners, that they may live.

Hence the Church and its pastors, its preachers, its gift of infallible truth, its Holy Scriptures, its sacraments, its sacrifice—all for the conversion of sinners, that they may live, "that they may have life, and may have it more abundantly" (John x. 10).

And hence, too, the manifold secret lights and promptings and helps called actual graces, by which the Holy Ghost is ever urging sinners to "turn from their way and live."

"Behold," says our Lord, "I stand at the door and knock. If any man shall hear my voice and open to me the door, I will come to him, and will sup with him, and he with me" (Apoc. iii. 20).

Our forgiveness, therefore, depends on an IF—*if* we "turn" to him; *if* we "be converted;" *if*, in short, we comply with God's conditions.

110. The Conditions of Forgiveness.— Infants who have never committed actual sin, are cleansed from original sin by simply being baptised; and there is needed no act of their own free will, nor any other condition whatsoever.

In adults, however, who are "taught of God" (John vi. 45), that is, taught by Christ, through His written word, or through His Church, God requires the following dispositions:—

(1) Faith, or a belief that God is; that He is the Rewarder of good and evil in a world to come; that God is Three in One; that Christ is God and Man; that He

died, as Man, and rose again to save us; and that all that He has taught us, by His written word and by His Church, is true. This is the meaning of the word "faith," or its equivalent, in every text of Scripture in which it is mentioned as a condition of pardon or justification. And it never means either *trust in Christ for personal salvation* or a *belief that Christ has already forgiven and justified us*, as some men try to make out.

(2) Fear of God's judgments and justice. "His mercy is upon them that fear Him" (Luke i. 50).

(3) Hope of pardon and grace here below, and of heaven hereafter, founded on the knowledge, given by faith, of what Christ has done and suffered for us, on the promises of God, and on His power and fidelity to keep them. "We are saved by Hope" (Rom. viii. 24).

(4) Love of God, or at least that beginning of love which consists in repentance, change of life, or the turning from sin to the serving of God, in order to escape His judgments and to merit His rewards.

(5) Hatred and detestation of all our mortal sins, and sorrow for having committed them, at least on account of the punishment they deserve.

(6) A strong resolution never to sin again.

(7) Consent to the prompting of the Holy Ghost, like that of the prodigal son, "I will arise and go to My Father" (Luke xv. 18).

(8) The due and valid reception of the sacrament of baptism, or of penance if baptism has been previously received; for these two sacraments are the ordinary, and as a rule the only means by which God blots out mortal sin.

(9) A will and intent to do penance for all sins committed after baptism. For "unless you do penance, you shall all likewise perish" (Luke xiii. 3).

This penance consists (1) in confessing our sins and performing the sacramental penance imposed at the confession, (2) in fasting and abstaining as the Church commands, (3) in obeying the Church and other lawful superiors, and (4) in submitting with patience and resignation to the trials, troubles and pains that Providence may send us.

111. Forgiveness.—When one that is in sin thus obeys the voice of the Holy Spirit, turns to God, and receives the sacrament of baptism or penance, or makes an act of love of God for His own sake, or an act of perfect contrition, with the will and intent to receive either baptism or penance as soon as possible, then God infallibly and instantaneously forgives his sins.

He not merely covers or hides them, and imputes to the sinful soul the justice or righteousness of Christ, as Luther and his followers asserted;

But He utterly blots them out, and makes the soul as free from the guilt of them as if it had never committed them.

112. Justification. — In freeing a repentant soul from sin, the Holy Ghost acts as follows :—

(1) He takes possession of the repentant soul, and begins to dwell within it. This He does by baptism or penance, as the Scriptures teach.

(2) His presence creates in the soul a "new creature" (Gal. vi. 15), a new quality or habit, which is called the righteousness or justice of God; not as being that righteousness by which God Himself is righteous, but as being a quality of soul created by God alone and not by any faith or works or good dispositions of ours.

(3) By taking possession of the soul, and by creating in it this "new creature," the Holy Ghost blots out sin, and decrees that the debt of eternal punishment due to it shall be cancelled then and for ever.

(4) By this twofold act—the infusion of grace and the driving out of sin—he makes the soul holy, or sanctifies it.

(5) And there and then, seeing his own "new creature," his own created holiness, righteousness, or justice—sanctifying grace as it is called—within

it, He pronounces it to be thereby holy, just or righteous; that is, to say, he formally justifies it.

All these things are done by one act of the Holy Spirit; and therefore they are commonly all included under the one term—Justification.

St. Paul expresses the order in which they are done in the following words: "Such were some of you (that is, grievous sinners); but ye are washed, but ye are sanctified, but ye are justified in the name of the Lord Jesus, and by the Spirit of our God" (1 Cor. vi. 11).

113. The Gift of the Holy Ghost.—It is clear from many texts that the justified Christian is made the temple of the Holy Ghost. For instance: "Repent," said St. Peter, "and be baptised every one of you in the name of Jesus Christ, for the remission of your sins; and you shall receive the gift of the Holy Ghost" (Acts ii. 38).

But the Holy Ghost is the uncreated love of the Father and the Son. Therefore where He is, there also must the Father and the Son be (John xiv. 20; xvii. 20—23; 1 John iii. 24).

Accordingly this glorious privilege which a justified soul has of possessing God is spoken of in Scripture in very many phrases, as for instance,—"Your members are the temple of the Holy Ghost, Who is in you, Whom you have from God" (1 Cor. vi. 19); "You are the temple of the living God" (2 Cor. vi. 16); "a holy temple in the Lord, in whom you also are built together into a habitation of God in the Spirit" (Eph. ii. 22); "Christ in you the hope of glory" (Col. i. 27); "Know ye not that Christ Jesus is in you?" (2 Cor. xiii. 5), &c., &c.

And lastly, St. Paul founds all his argument in Romans viii., on the fact that "the Spirit of God," (Whom he also calls "the Spirit of Christ," for the Holy Ghost proceeds from the Father *and* the Son) was dwelling in those to whom he wrote (*see v.* 9) he speaks of the Spirit aiding our weakness and praying for us with unspeakable groanings (*v.* 26); and he adds that those whom God *foreknew* and *predestined* (to be made) *conformable to the image of his Son* by patience in suffering, those *he has called* to the faith, and *justified*, and *glorified* (*v.* 29, 30).

By the word "glorified" he recalls the visible presence of the glory of God, called in the Targums the Shechinah, the miraculous flame of fire that dwelt in the tabernacle and afterwards in Solomon's Temple; to which also St. John seems to refer, when he says, "And the Word was made flesh, and dwelt (or *tabernacled*) amongst us; and we saw his *glory*" and the rest (John i. 14).

Such then is the truly "glorious" privilege of a justified soul, to be made like Christ Himself, the temple, the tabernacle, of God, and the place where His glory dwells.

114. Sanctifying Grace, or the Righteousness of God.—(1) Habitual or sanctifying grace is the "new creature" or "new creation" formed within us by the supernatural presence of the Holy Ghost.

It makes us children and friends of God, not in name only, but in fact.

It makes us righteous, holy, pleasing to God.

It gives us a right, which God has recognised, to be saved from hell and taken to heaven.

And it gives to all our good works, our acts of obedience and acts of devotion, a supernatural worth or value for which God will give us an eternal reward.

(2) This justice or righteousness of God is called "grace" because it is given *gratis*, being a pure gift of God.

We can do nothing to really deserve it; we can pay God no price for it; we cannot buy it by any act of ours however good.

We can only open our souls for it, so to speak, by believing, hoping, fearing, repenting, and receiving baptism, or confessing our sins; as a beggar may open his hand to receive the free gift of a passer-by.

It has been merited for us by our Saviour's Passion and Death, and by that alone.

So a justified soul is said to be "redeemed," that is, bought back unto God, and reclaimed from the power of the devil, "by the precious Blood of Christ" (1 Peter i. 19)

(3) Sanctifying Grace, or the Righteousess of God, which is also spoken of in scripture as a *sealing* (Eph. iv. 30), as *life* (John x. 10), and elsewhere as *light*, *seed*, the *pledge* of future glory, an *anointing* of the Holy One, &c., has been merited for us by Christ and given to us by the Holy Ghost.

So St. Paul teaches that all the justified are "justified freely by his *grace* through the redemption that is in Christ Jesus" (Rom. iii. 24); and again that "the Charity of God has been poured into our hearts by the Holy Ghost, Who has been given to us" (v. 5).

(4) The Righteousness of God or sanctifying grace first comes to the soul in baptism.

It is driven from the soul by wilful mortal sin.

It may be re-acquired in the sacrament of penance.

And it is to be kept, increased and strengthened by prayer, the reception of the Sacraments and other good works.

So St. Paul says, "In Christ Jesus neither circumcision availeth anything, nor uncircumcision; but faith, *which worketh by charity*" (Gal. v. 6);

And again, "Circumcision is nothing, and uncircumcision is nothing; but *the keeping of the commandments of God*" (1 Cor. vii. 19).

(5) The chief effect of sanctifying grace is to make us love God above all things for the sake of His own great goodness: and this is Charity.

A soul therefore in the state of grace has always Charity—that is at least the power and disposition to love God more than all things, and that not merely for the sake of what He will do for us, but for the sake of what He is in Himself.

So Charity and Grace are practically one and the same thing, and both are included in Scripture under either name alone.

115. The Infused Virtues.—The Holy Ghost gives us at our justification, together with sanctifying grace, certain good dispositions, which empower, incline and dispose us to do good acts.

These good dispositions are called *Infused Virtues*.

Thus Faith, Hope and Charity are infused, or poured into our souls at our baptism.

So are Prudence, Justice, Fortitude and Temperance, with all the virtues that hang, as it were, upon them.

Our Blessed Lord also mentions eight states of virtue, that have attached to them each a special blessedness, or foretaste of the sweetness of heaven; for which reason they are called the *Eight Beatitudes* (See Matt. v. 3—10).

So with sanctifying grace we receive the power and the disposition—to be poor in spirit or detached from earthly things, to be meek, to mourn for sin, to long for righteousness, to show mercy, to be pure in thought, to be lovers of peace, and to be patient under crosses and persecutions.

These are so many modes of Charity, or ways of loving God and our neighbour.

There is given us therefore, with sanctifying grace, a power and disposition to observe the whole law of God.

116. The Seven Gifts of the Spirit.—As indwelling aids to the exercise of Faith, Hope and Charity, and to help us to bring forth the fruit of the Spirit, the Holy Ghost gives us also, with sanctifying grace, the sevenfold spirit that was first poured forth upon the soul of Christ (see Isaias xi. 1—3):—

The spirit of Wisdom, to enable us to judge rightly in matters that affect salvation;

The spirit of Understanding, to grasp the mysteries of faith;

The spirit of Counsel, to choose better and more

meritorious ways of serving God, especially by means of poverty, chastity and obedience, whether in the world or in the cloister;

The spirit of Fortitude, to be brave and all-enduring in the struggle for eternal life;

The spirit of Knowledge, to know God and the truths of religion;

The spirit of Piety, to be loving children of God;

And the spirit of the Fear of the Lord, to be anxious and careful never to offend Him.

The Gifts of the Holy Ghost are always given with sanctifying grace,

And they are greatly increased and strengthened in the sacrament of confirmation.

117. The Helping Influences of the Holy Ghost, or Actual Graces.—Whenever we act with the intention of pleasing God, or in other words, do anything for our soul's salvation, either *before* we are justified or *after*, the Holy Ghost helps us.

He helps us by acts, which are called actual graces.

Thus He first enlightens us, as to what we ought to do; as for instance, to pray, to resist a temptation, or to obey a commandment;

Then He gives us an impulse to do it;

And if we consent, He helps us further in our doing of it.

Without actual grace we could not do properly and with right intention any of the good works that conduce to salvation.

So God gives to all—even to the most obstinate sinners—*enough* actual grace *at least* to enable them to save their souls.

And the more we yield to grace, and do good deeds, the more knowledge of what is right and the more help to do it will the Holy Ghost give us.

118. Good Works.—A good work is any act, whether of mind or body, by which our Faith, Hope, or Charity towards God or our neighbour is exercised.

A good work is therefore an act which is agreeable to right reason, or not forbidden by the law of God, done freely, and in some way done for God.

Or a good work is anything we do that pleases God.

Good Works, as a rule, belong to one of three kinds, Prayer, Fasting, or Alms-deeds.

Prayer includes all worship of God, both in secret, as by internal acts of Faith, Hope and Charity, and in public, as by assisting at Mass, Benediction, or other service of the Church.

Fasting includes all acts of self-mortification.

And Alms-deeds include acts of kindness, and all benefits done to another.

Some good works we are commanded to do, either by our Lord Jesus Christ or by His Church.

And some we may do or not do, just as we please.

But for all of them, if we do them for God, He will give us a great reward.

119. The Merit or the Reward of Good Works.—(1) *Before* justification, that is while in the state of sin, we can only pray and repent of our sins and receive a sacrament, and so move and allow God's mercy to give us pardon and grace.

In justification God gives us with pardon and grace a right to enter heaven, and to receive some reward, which is called by theologians the first degree of glory.

After justification we can, by the help of actual grace, really merit an increase of grace and charity in this life and a corresponding increase of reward and glory in the world to come.

We thus increase our righteousness and earn a heavenly reward by our every act of obedience to the commandments of God, or of the Church, or of the state, or of any lawful superior; by our every act of virtue; by our every resistance to temptation; by our every occupation; in short by every single thing we do (except sin of course), provided the act be in some way done for God, or in some way offered to Him, and so made an act of worship.

Let us therefore say frequently the following or some such act of offering:—

> O My God to thee I offer
> All I think or do or say,
> With what Jesus did to please Thee;
> Keep me, Lord, from sin this day.

(2) If, having done good works in grace, we fall into mortal sin, we lose all the merit of those good works.

But if we afterwards repent, their merit returns to us.

So in heaven, if we get there, we shall have a reward for every good act we did for God in the state of grace.

Though in hell, if we die in mortal sin, we shall only be punished for sins unrepented of, and not for any that God has once forgiven.

(3) We can merit in some sense for others also.

For by praying and offering our good works for them we can obtain them, if God so wills it, perseverance in virtue, and efficacious actual graces that will lead them to the faith, to conversion, to repentance.

"Pray one for another that you may be saved" (James v. 16).

(4) Of course the better the work is in itself—the better the purpose for which we do it—the more love towards God we exercise in doing it—and above all, the more closely our souls are united to the Holy Ghost by grace and charity when we do it, the more meritorious the act will be.

120. The Temporal Punishment due to Sin.—For sin that has been forgiven, the sinner must suffer, like David (see 2 Kings xii. and xxiv.) some temporal punishment.

The temporal punishment must be endured (1) in reparation to the offended Majesty of God, and (2) for the thorough cleansing of the soul.

We can really suffer this punishment in purgatory only.

But we can suffer on earth other punishment instead of it; which is called doing penance, or making satisfaction.

121. Satisfaction.—To man in his fallen state good works are naturally hard and troublesome.

They have therefore the nature of punishment.

So by doing good works we punish ourselves for our sins, and escape the torments of purgatory.

In other words, good works are satisfactory so far forth as they are hard or painful or troublesome.

And some, like fasting, obedience and bodily mortification, are more troublesome or painful than others; and are therefore the more satisfactory.

122. Vicarious Satisfaction.—As we can offer the merit of our good works for each other,

So we can obtain the remission of each other's temporal punishment by offering to God our own sufferings and penances for this intention.

And this we can do not only for living people, but also for the souls in purgatory.

123. Indulgences.—By virtue of the Communion of Saints, the Church has a treasure of satisfactions.

For our Lord's satisfactions were infinite;

Those of the saints were much greater than they needed for the cleansing of their own souls;

And those of our Lady the Queen of Sorrows were not needed for herself at all, she being immaculate all her life.

So the Pope has power (see Matt. xvi. 19) to give us the benefit of all these satisfactions;

And he does so by granting Indulgences.

An Indulgence is therefore a remission of temporal punishment, granted by the Church, apart from any sacrament, in virtue of the superabundant satisfactions of our Lord and of the saints.

Indulgences are granted for the doing of certain good works.

For some the Indulgence is *plenary*, or equal to a full and complete satisfaction, or a remission of the whole temporal punishment that the soul would otherwise have to endure.

For other good works the Indulgence is *partial*, and is equal to the amount of temporal punishment that would have been remitted, or rather cancelled, by so many days or years of ancient canonical penance.

Thus "Forty days' Indulgence" means a cancelling of as much temporal punishment as would be cancelled by a penance of forty days in the old canonical style.

Indulgences are applicable by way of *suffrage*, or *petition*, for the souls in purgatory.

To gain an Indulgence, we must (1) do the work, or works, prescribed, and (2) be in the state of grace, at least when the last of them is done.

124. The Power of Prayer. — Prayer is meritorious and satisfactory, like any other good work.

But besides, it has a power all its own.

It is a direct appeal to God's own goodness—to the loving kindness of our Almighty Father.

It is therefore the most profitable and the most necessary of all good works.

By prayer we can obtain for ourselves and for others both merit or glory in heaven, and the cancelling of temporal punishment, with numberless blessings and favours for soul and body.

For our Blessed Lord has said, "Ask and it shall be given you; seek and ye shall find; knock and it shall be opened unto you" (Matt. vii. 7).

125. Summary of the Tenth Article.— In the Church of God there is Forgiveness of Sins for all that apply for it with due dispositions.

Original sin is forgiven in baptism.

Mortal sin is forgiven in baptism, or in penance, or by perfect contrition.

Venial sin is forgiven by any sacrament, sacramental, or other good work done for God in the state of grace.

And after the sin is forgiven, we may obtain the remission of the temporal punishment:—

(1) By sacramental satisfaction, or the penance that is given in confession;
(2) By the fasting and abstinence appointed by the Church;
(3) By acts of obedience to parents and lawful superiors;
(4) By voluntary mortifications, especially by keeping away from the pleasurable occasions of sin;
(5) By patiently bearing any sickness, injury, loss, or misfortune, in union with the sufferings of Christ;
(6) By gaining indulgences;
(7) By great contrition;
(8) By prayer.

Thus there is in the Church of God Forgiveness of Sins, original and actual, mortal and venial, both as to guilt and to punishment eternal and temporal, for all who properly apply for it.

126. What Justification does not do.—It does not restore us entirely to the first happy state of man before his fall.

It restores to us indeed the possession of the Holy Ghost, charity and grace; but it does not restore to us the perfect beauty and perfect health of body, nor the great natural knowledge and intelligence, nor the perfect control and right ordering of the will and affections, nor the freedom of the body from pain, disease, decay and death, nor the freedom of the soul from sorrow, which the first man had together with grace, but which he forfeited by sin.

These gifts will be restored to the saints alone at the restoration of all things on the judgment day.

For the present our souls, though justified, are afflicted by nature with ignorance, malice, weakness for good, proneness to evil and liability to sorrow.

And our bodies are subject to pain, decay, disease, and finally to death.

127. Death and Judgment.—Death is the separation of the soul from the body.

"It is appointed unto men once to die, and after this the judgment" (Heb. ix. 27).

We must therefore all die, though we know not the day nor the hour.

And immediately after death we shall be judged.

Then our soul will be sentenced—either to hell, if guilty of mortal sin; or to purgatory, if in grace yet tainted with sin; or to heaven, if pure and free from sinful stain.

And the soul having gone, the body will decay and return to dust.

ELEVENTH ARTICLE OF THE CREED.

The Resurrection of the Body.

128. The End of the World.—The Gospel will first be preached in every land. The Jews will have been converted to Jesus Christ. Then charity will grow cold, and faith be nearly lost. There will be wars, famines, plagues, earthquakes, and a darkness of the sun, moon and stars. Antichrist will persecute the Church, and reign on the earth three years and a half. Enoch the patriarch and Elias the prophet will return to bear witness to Christ, and be put to death by Antichrist. And at last a great fire will burn the world.

129. The Second Coming of Christ.—Then the sign of the Son of Man, the Cross, shall appear in heaven,

And Christ shall come in the clouds in great power and majesty.

"And He shall send His angels with a trumpet, and a great voice; and they shall gather together His elect from the four winds, from the farthest parts of the heavens to the utmost bounds of them" (Matt. xxiv. 31).

130. The Rising of the Dead.—Then "the trumpet shall sound and the dead shall arise incorruptible;"

"For this corruptible must put on incorruption, and this mortal must put on immortality" (1 Cor. xv. 52, 53).

All will rise again.

The souls of the wicked will come from hell, and the souls of the righteous will come from heaven, to be united once more and for ever, each to its own body.

And all, both good and bad, will appear in the flesh before the Lord.

131. The General Judgment.—Then every man's work will be judged. And sentence will be passed upon us for every thought, word, deed, or omission of our whole lives.

To those who have been wicked our Blessed Lord will say,—"Depart from Me ye cursed into everlasting fire which was prepared for the devil and his angels" (Matt. xxv. 41).

And to the good,—"Come ye blessed of My Father, possess ye the Kingdom prepared for you" (Matt. xxv. 34).

TWELFTH ARTICLE OF THE CREED.

132. Life Everlasting.—From the day of judgment our bodies and souls will be united for ever.

They will be punished together in hell, or rewarded together in heaven.

The bodies of the righteous will be glorified, and will have these four gifts or qualities—

(1) *Impassibility*, or freedom from all pain and suffering;

(2) *Agility*, or the power of moving swiftly as thought from one part of creation to another;

(3) *Subtilty*, by which they will be, as it were, spiritualized and freed from their present grossness and encumbrances;

(4) *Brightness* and brilliancy; for as the soul will shine with the light and splendour of grace, so the body will shine for ever with the glory of the soul.

CHAPTER III.
HOPE AND PRAYER.

133. The Grounds of Hope.—We are taught by Faith that God is merciful; that He wishes us all to be saved; that He gave His Son Jesus to die for our salvation; that He is faithful to His promises and able to fulfil them; and that He has promised, in view of the merits of Christ, to give us eternal life, on condition that we keep His commandments.

These and such like truths of Faith are the grounds of the virtue of Hope.

Hope, then, is a firm expectation, founded (1) on Faith and (2) on our own determination to keep the commandments, that God will give us life everlasting in heaven, and all the grace that is needed upon earth to enable us to obtain it.

Hope is as necessary for salvation as Faith is; for St. Paul says, "We are saved by Hope" (Rom. viii. 24).

And like Faith, it is a gift of God, infused into our souls in baptism.

The virtue of Hope is manifested, exercised and strengthened by Prayer.

134. Prayer, in the wider meaning of the word, is any pious raising of the mind to God, either in worship, or in contemplation of His glory and His works, or in imploring pardon, grace, and other favours.

More strictly it is the raising up of our minds and hearts to God, to commend to Him our needs and desires. In this sense prayer is Hope and desire reverently manifested.

135. The Necessity of Prayer.—We may pray with our mind alone, or we may speak our prayer with our lips; we may pray in secret, or in the congregation of the faithful; but pray we must, for God has made it a condition of our salvation that we ask His grace in prayer.

The necessity of Prayer arises from the following facts:—

(1) That by our natural powers alone we can do nothing conducive to our salvation. We need God's helping grace,—
>To rise from sin,
>To resist temptation,
>To keep in a state of grace,
>And to do meritorious good works.

(2) That helping grace is a free gift of God. He can give it or not, as He pleases, and give it on what condition He pleases.

(3) That He chooses to give it, as a rule, only to those that humble themselves before Him and ask it of Him.

The first helping grace He gives is indeed an unasked gift; but, as a rule, that grace is the grace *to pray;* and in answer to prayer all further grace is given.

God brings the sinner who prays nearer to justification.

And the just man who prays He strengthens in Faith, Hope, Charity, Humility, Purity, and other virtues, according to the needs and prayers of the suppliant.

Thus all have need to pray—sinners to get free from their sin, and the righteous to preserve their righteousness.

136. The Times and Seasons proper for Prayer.—Our Blessed Lord taught that "we ought always to pray" (Luke xviii. 1); and St. Paul says, "Pray without ceasing" (1 Thes. v. 17).

We ought therefore to pray frequently.

Particularly we ought to pray in the seasons of Lent and Advent; on Sundays and great feast days; in moments of temptation or affliction; and whenever we have any special need of God's assistance.

Moreover, the custom of all good Catholics is to pray the first thing in the morning and the last thing at night, and to say "grace" before and after meals.

137. Objects of Prayer. — We are bound under pain of mortal sin to pray for all those graces that are necessary for our salvation.

These we must ask for unconditionally, for God wishes all to have them and therefore all to pray for them.

We may also pray for temporal goods, both for ourselves and for others; for health, prosperity, success in honest business, and the like.

But these we must ask for a good purpose only, with the glory of God in view, and with submission to the Divine will.

"Seek ye first the kingdom of God and His justice, and all these things shall be added to you" (Matt. vi. 33).

138. Dispositions for Prayer. — In order that our prayers may surely be heard, we should pray with those good dispositions which, as scripture informs us, make prayer agreeable to God.

We should therefore pray: —

(1) With our hearts prepared, that is, mindful of the importance of the work we are about to perform.

(2) With our souls free from sin; "For the eyes of the Lord are upon the *just*, and His ears unto their prayers" (Psalm xxxiii. 16).

(3) For objects conducive to salvation; first, indeed, for the pardon of our sins, especially if guilty of mortal sin, and chiefly, afterwards, for grace to avoid sin and serve God for the future.

(4) With gratitude for past favours and many acts of thanksigving for them.

(5) With attention and fervour, banishing distractions, at least to the best of our power.

(6) With humility; making our prayer an acknowledgment of our poverty, baseness, uselessness, and dependence upon the bounty of God. "God resisteth the proud, and giveth His grace to the humble" (James iv. 6). It is chiefly the humility that is exercised in prayer, that makes prayer an act of worship.

(7) With unbounded confidence in God's power and goodness and willingness to help us. "Ask in faith, nothing wavering" (James i 6).

(8) With resignation and submission to the will of God. For God in His wisdom may see it best sometimes to answer prayer immediately, sometimes to delay, and sometimes to grant us, especially in temporal matters, not precisely what we ask, but something better. In all things we must allow God to know best, and bow to His holy will.

(9) With perseverance and a holy importunity, like the friend in the parable (Luke xi. 8), and the woman of Chanaan (Matt. xv. 22—28). It is "the *continual* prayer of the just," that "availeth much;" (James v. 16); and no man has a right to "set a time to the mercy of the Lord" (see Judith viii. 13).

(10) In the name and through the merits of Christ; for "Whatsoever you shall ask the Father in My name, that will I do," was the promise of our Blessed Lord (John xiv. 13). So the Church ends all her prayers— "Through Christ our Lord. Amen."

(11) Invoking the aid of the Blessed in heaven.

(12) In union, and when we can, in company, with each other; for our Lord says, "If two of you shall agree upon earth concerning anything whatsoever they shall ask, it shall be done for them by My Father who is in heaven. For where there are two or three gathered together in My name there am I in the midst of them" (Matt. xviii. 19, 20). And hence there is a special value in the public prayers of the Church.

139. Intercession, or Intercessory Prayer, is prayer offered for other people.

Those that have charge of others' souls, as pastors, parents, masters, and mistresses, teachers, &c., are bound in justice, as well as in charity, to pray for those under their charge.

By the virtue of charity we are all obliged to "pray for one another" (James v. 16).

We must pray especially for the Pope and for the Church; "for kings and for all that are in high stations" (1 Tim. ii 2); and also for our parents, relations, superiors, benefactors, friends and enemies—even "for them that persecute and calumniate" us (Matt. v. 44).

Zeal for God's honour will prompt us to pray for the conversion of sinners, the perseverance of the good, the propagation of the faith, and the good of our country.

And all English-speaking Catholics have some obligation to pray for the conversion of England.

It is also "a holy and wholesome thought to pray for the dead that they may be loosed from sins" (2 Mach. xii. 46).

All the obligation of intercessory prayer may be fulfilled by the simple recitation of the "Our Father" and the "Hail Mary" with the proper intentions.

140. The Invocation of Saints.—It is good and useful to ask the saints and angels to pray for us.

There are many proofs in Scripture that they know our needs, and can help us by their prayer (for instance, Luke xv. 10, and Zach. i. 12).

They are friends of God, and have one sole desire, that is, that God's will may be done.

And since God wills that we should save our souls, His Saints have an interest in our salvation.

The angels, as Scripture teaches, and especially our angel guardians, are charged,—

To inspire us with good thoughts,

To guard us from evil,
To help us in temporal matters,
And to pray for our spiritual welfare.

Our Patron Saints perform for us similar offices.

And Mary, the Mother of Jesus, the most blessed among women, and the most grace-endowed of all creatures, because of her nearness, dearness and special love to Jesus, and because of the part she played in our redemption, has (1) a special interest in our salvation, and (2) a special power to intercede on our behalf.

And therefore, besides praying to God ourselves, we should also seek the help of those whom He so much loves, whose prayers he delights to answer, and whom He Himself has made our advocates.

Note.—It is worth observing (1) that the saints are able to help us *solely* because they are those that " have washed their robes," &c., and " have made them white in the blood of the Lamb;" that is, because they are the first fruits of the mediation of Christ; (2) that so, their power of interceding owes its very existence to the mediation of Christ; (3) that the seeking of their intercession is therefore a homage to the mediation of Christ; and (4) that of all the wild notions brought in by Protestantism, perhaps the most absurd was this—that our Lord's mediation was dishonoured or superseded by our seeking the intercession of the saints.

141. The Efficacy of Prayer.—Prayer offered with proper dispositions is always heard, as is clear from the promise of Christ.

He has said, " Ask and you shall receive " (John xvi. 24); and " Everyone that asketh receiveth " (Matt. vii. 8).

Than these words there can be no more solemn assurance.

142. The Lord's Prayer and its Explanation.—The best of all prayers is the prayer which our Blessed Saviour taught.

This prayer is a summary of all that God wishes us all to pray for.

We must know it by heart and understand its meaning.

The "Lord's Prayer" is as follows:—

Our Father Who art in heaven;
Hallowed be Thy name;
Thy kingdom come;
Thy will be done on earth as it is in heaven;
Give us this day our daily bread;
And forgive us our trespasses, as we forgive them that trespass against us;
And lead us not into temptation;
But deliver us from evil. Amen.

In this prayer our Lord has taught us to call God our "Father," because He is the Father of all by creation, and especially the Father of Christians by baptism.

He has taught us to say "Our" Father, not "My" Father, because we must pray for all children of God, and not for ourselves only.

"*Hallowed be Thy name,*" or blessed be Thy name, is a prayer that God's name may never be blasphemed, but that He may be known, praised, loved and served by all men.

"*Thy kingdom come,*" is a prayer that God may reign as king in all our hearts, that He may reign by the spread of His Church throughout the world, and that we may one day reign with Him for ever in heaven.

"*Thy will be done on earth, as it is in heaven,*" is a prayer that all men on earth, and we especially, may do God's will, that is, keep His commandments, with love, joy, delight and unswerving obedience, as the saints and angels do in heaven.

"*Give us this day our daily bread,*" is a prayer that God may give to us all whatever we need for soul and body; and the form of the petition suggests to us to pray each day for what we need for the day, trusting in God's Providence and care, without being too solicitous for the morrow (Matt. vi. 25—34)

"*Forgive us our trespasses, as we forgive them that trespass against us,*" is a prayer that God may forgive us our trespasses or sins, coupled with a protestation that we in our turn forgive all injuries from our hearts. For we know that unless we forgive our fellow men, God will not forgive us (see Matt. xviii. 35).

"*Lead us not into temptation,*" is a prayer that God may guard us, and keep us away from bad company and from all occasions of sin, and may give us His grace never to yield to any suggestions of the devil, the world, or the flesh.

"*Deliver us from evil,*" is a prayer that God may keep us safe from the devil, who is the evil one; from sin, which is the great evil; from everything which He knows is or would be for us an evil, that is, an occasion of sin; and also from temporal misfortune.

143. The "Hail Mary," or Angelic Salutation.—After the "Our Father," all Catholics say the "Hail Mary." This prayer consists of three parts:—(1) Of some words of the Angel Gabriel to the Blessed Virgin Mary at the Annunciation (Luke i. 28); (2) of some words of St. Elizabeth addressed to our Lady on the occasion of her visit to St. Elizabeth (Luke i. 42); and (3) of an invocation or prayer added by the Church.

Gabriel's words were, "Hail! full of grace, the Lord is with thee, blessed art thou amongst women."

St. Elizabeth's words were, "Blessed art thou amongst women; and blessed is the fruit of thy womb."

All the other words have been added by the Church. The whole Prayer runs thus:—

"*Hail, Mary, full of grace, the Lord is with thee, blessed art thou amongst women, and blessed is the fruit of thy womb, Jesus. Holy Mary, Mother of God, pray for us sinners, now, and at the hour of our death. Amen.*"

"*Hail,*" means, "I salute thee."

"*Full of grace,*" implies that Mary was immaculately conceived, and without sin throughout her life.

"*The Lord is with thee,*" denotes her perfect possession of God.

"*Blessed art thou amongst women,*" denotes the height of her dignity: being purer than all creatures; being chosen to be the Mother of God; and yet, by a stupendous miracle, not ceasing to be a Virgin.

"*The fruit of thy womb,*" means "thy child,"— Jesus, who was blessed, not with an imparted blessedness like that of His Mother, but with a blessedness infinite and all His own, because He was God.

In the last part we ask her to pray for us *now* and at *the hour of death*, the two most important moments of our life, and the only two of which we can be sure.

This prayer is thus a hymn, first, according to the words, in honour of Mary, and secondly, but yet more truly, in honour of Jesus; for all the honour that is in it given to Mary is through and for Jesus her Son.

144. Meditation or Mental Prayer.—Prayers that are said with the lips and voice and consist of a set form of words, are called vocal prayers.

But another most excellent way of prayer is meditation or mental prayer.

The essence of meditation is to think about God, or some truth of faith, or any words of Holy Scripture, that may move us to pious affections towards Him.

A simple method of meditation is,—

(1) Ask God's grace to help us;

(2) To read a passage in the Gospels or in some meditation book;

(3) To close the book and think about what we have read;

(4) To speak to our Lord the good thoughts that arise in our minds;

And (5) to make good resolutions.

CHAPTER IV.
CHARITY.

145. The Meaning of the word Charity is dearness or love.

Among Christians it means (1) the love of God for His own sake, and (2) the love of our neighbour for God's sake.

It is the greatest of all the virtues; for of Faith, Hope and Charity, "the greatest of these is Charity" (1 Cor. xiii. 13).

146. The Two Precepts of Charity.—Our Blessed Lord has said, "Thou shalt love the Lord thy God with thy whole heart, and with thy whole soul, and with thy whole mind. This is the greatest and first commandment. And the second is like to this:—Thou shalt love thy neighbour as thyself" (Matt. xxii. 37—39).

Therefore Charity is absolutely necessary for salvation.

147. The Love of God.—Charity, or the love which we must have for God, is a disposition of the will, by which we cleave to God, by which we think and say and do that which pleases Him, and renounce whatever displeases Him, at least in any serious matter, not merely because we hope to be rewarded for pleasing Him, or fear to be punished for offending Him, but chiefly because God is Goodness Itself, and worthy, for being what He is, to be loved and served.

In other words, Charity is a deliberate choice of the will, in view of God's infinite Goodness, to give ourselves wholly up to Him, to live to do His will, and to lose or suffer anything, even to die, rather than to offend Him, *at least by mortal sin.*

"*At least by mortal sin;*" for there are three degrees of Charity.

In the first, we renounce, for God's sake, all mortal sin; and this degree is absolutely necessary for salvation.

In the second, we renounce, for God's sake, even venial sin; and this degree of Charity is much more pleasing to Him.

In the third, we wish Him, for His own sake, all praise, adoration, honour, and glory, and endeavour ourselves to do that which is best and most pleasing to Him.

To love God thus is perfect Charity.

Thus Charity is a practical love of God, consisting of inward affection and its outward expression.

Our Charity may often be made manifest to us by a feeling of devotion, a sweet and sensible attraction of our souls to God, a yearning after Him, and even a desire, like St. Paul's, to be dissolved and to be with Christ (Phil. i. 23).

But this devotional feeling is not commanded; and in fact, as may be seen in the lives of the Saints, perfect Charity may exist, at least for a time, without it.

The Virtue of Charity, or the disposition to love God more than all other things, is, like Faith and Hope, a gift of God, infused into our souls in justification, or, as St. Paul says, "poured out into our hearts by the Hóly Ghost, who is given to us" (Rom. v. 5).

Charity always exists in the soul, together with sanctifying grace.

Together with grace it is driven from the soul by mortal sin.

And together with grace it may be regained, either in the Sacrament of Penance, or by an Act of Contrition.

148. The Motives of Charity.—(1) We are bound to love God, chiefly for His own sake, or because He is what He is—the Eternal and Living

Truth, Wisdom, Righteousness, Purity, Mercy, Goodness and Charity, worthy in Himself of all love and worship.

(2) We are bound to love Him "because He first loved us" (1 John iv. 19), having created us, redeemed us by the Precious Blood of Christ, and given us graces and blessings without number.

(3) We are bound to love Him because He alone can give everlasting life, and because apart from Him we should be miserable for ever.

We are bound to love God for His own sake; for if we kept His commandments *merely* for the sake of His reward, or to escape hell-fire, our cleaving to God would be good indeed, so far as it went, but would not be Charity.

Nevertheless, "the fear of the Lord is the beginning of wisdom" (Ps. cx. 10); and we are bidden to "lay up for" ourselves "treasures in heaven" (Mat. vi. 20), and "so to run that" we "may obtain an incorruptible crown" (1 Cor. ix. 24 and 25).

So at one and the same time we may fear God's punishments, hope for a reward in heaven, and yet love God so truly for His own sake, that even if we knew of no heaven to hope for, and no hell to fear, we should love Him and serve Him all the same.

149. Charity in Act.—St. Paul says "Whether you eat or drink, or whatsoever else you do, do all things for the glory of God" (1 Cor. x. 31).

By this precept we are bound (1) to avoid sin, and (2) to refer our chief actions in some way to God.

That is, as Christians, we ought to take care never to do anything which is sinful, that is, either wrong in itself, or wrong under the circumstances, or wrong through being done for a bad end or motive.

Hence all our deliberate acts should be either the observance of positive law, as hearing Mass on Sundays; or acts of virtue, not then and there commanded, as hearing Mass on a week-day, saying grace at meals, or denying ourselves some lawful pleasure; or acts which are naturally good, that is, tend in some way to the well-being, comfort, or lawful enjoyment of ourselves or others, such as eating, drinking, labouring, or taking needful amusement, in which there is no sin: and all these acts, which are naturally good, may be turned into acts of Charity, if done in grace and done for God.

As Christians, of course, we are supposed and expected to be always in the state of grace, that is, to have Charity in our souls, and so to be living "temples of God" (1 Cor. iii. 16).

And this being so, it is well, at least once a day, but the oftener the better, to offer to God, in union with the acts and sufferings of Jesus, all we think or say, do or suffer.

By every act thus offered, we give glory to God, increase our grace and Charity, merit a reward, and obtain pardon of venial sins and remission of temporal punishment.

150. The Growth of Charity.—The first germ of Charity is the gift of God.

This first germ of Charity may be strengthened, increased, made, so to speak, to grow:—

(1) By continual prayer—"O, my God, teach me to love Thee in time and eternity;"

(2) By making Acts of Charity;

(3) By striving to do all things for the greater glory of God;

(4) By denying ourselves, that is, by resisting and curbing all those inclinations which tend to lead us into mortal or venial sin, or to hinder us from doing what we know to be most pleasing to God;

(5) By thinking often of God's infinite goodness;

(6) By reading the Holy Scripture, and lovingly pondering in our hearts, like Mary (Luke ii. 19 and 51), the words and actions of our Blessed Lord; and thus learning to know Him, as He lived and loved us and showed us His glory and His goodness in His human nature;

(7) By studying, especially in the New Testament, how the Saints, like Mary His Mother, St. Joseph, the Magdalene, Peter, Paul, Stephen, and John loved Him, and by begging their prayers that we may be followers of them, as they were of Christ (1 Cor. iv. 16).

151. The Second Precept of Charity binds us (1) to love ourselves, and (2) to love our neighbours as ourselves, for God's sake.

152. The Love of Ourselves. — We are bound to love ourselves (1) because it is natural to do so, and (2) because of God's positive command to do so.

But we are bound to love ourselves with a reasonable love, and for motives supplied by faith.

These motives are: (1) because we are children of God, made to His image and likeness, redeemed by the Precious Blood of Jesus, and therefore very dear to His Sacred Heart; and (2) because He has made us for His own glory, as well as for our happiness.

Now by natural self-love, rightly ordered, we desire for ourselves such things as health, strength, long life, the goodwill of men, peace, plenty, joy, and harmless pleasure. We desire that other people may treat us kindly, overlook our failings, and give us credit for meaning well.

But by spiritual self-love we desire things that are good for our souls, such as grace and Charity, and all the virtues; such as means and opportunities for doing good, for sanctifying our souls, and for laying up treasures in heaven; and such only of the good things of this life as will not hinder us from increasing our merit in heaven.

153. The Love of Our Neighbours, or Brotherly Love.—We are commanded to love our neighbours as ourselves.

All men and women are neighbours and brethren.

We are therefore bound by the virtue of Charity

to love strangers, pagans, infidels, heretics, Protestants, Jews, Catholics, bad and good, friends and enemies.

For all these, like ourselves, are children of God; all bear His image, at least by creation; and all have been redeemed by the Precious Blood of Christ.

But especially we are bound to love those whom God has made our neighbours in a special sense, namely, parents, kindred, friends, and benefactors, our fellow countrymen, and those that belong to the "household of the Faith" (Gal. vi. 10), that is, Catholics.

The precept of loving our neighbour is especially the precept of the Gospel.

For our Lord says, "A *new commandment* I give unto you: that you love one another; as I have loved you, that you also love one another (John xiii. 34).

And He adds, "For this shall men know that you are My disciples, if you love one another."

To fulfil this precept we are not bound to love anyone as much as we love ourselves; but we are bound to love all men as truly as we love ourselves, and to love them in the same manner and for the same supernatural motives as we love ourselves.

We must love them with a practical love, that is (1) by wishing them well and praying for them, as we do when we say the Lord's Prayer; (2) by giving them aid, both of soul and body, according as they need it and we can give it; and (3) by forgiving the injuries they do us.

154. God's Will in Detail is made known to us:—
(1) By the Ten Commandments;
(2) By the teaching and examples of Christ;
(3) By the commandments of the Church;
(4) By the Evangelical Counsels, for such as have the grace, the will, and the opportunity.

CHAPTER V.
THE DECALOGUE,
OR TEN COMMANDMENTS.

I. I am the Lord thy God, who brought thee out of the land of Eygpt, and out of the house of bondage. Thou shalt not have strange gods before Me. Thou shalt not make to thyself any graven thing, nor the likeness of anything that is in heaven above, or in the earth beneath, nor of those things that are in the waters under the earth. Thou shalt not adore them nor serve them.

II. Thou shalt not take the name of the Lord Thy God in vain.

III. Remember that thou keep holy the Sabbath Day.

IV. Honour thy father and thy mother.

V. Thou shalt not kill.

VI. Thou shalt not commit adultery.

VII. Thou shalt not steal.

VIII. Thou shalt not bear false witness against thy neighbour.

IX. Thou shalt not covet thy neighbour's wife.

X. Thou shalt not covet thy neighbour's goods.

155. God wrote these ten Commandments on two tables of stone, and gave them to Moses, amid thunder and lightning, upon Mount Sinai (Ex. xx).

They tell us the first principles of the natural moral law.

The actions they forbid are sins;

The actions they command are good works.

All men are able, with the help of God's grace, to keep the Commandments.

And all men are bound to keep them (1) because they are natural laws, and reasonable rules of conduct, (2) because Jesus Christ has given them forth anew, and explained them in detail, and (3) because He has said, "If thou wilt enter into life, keep the commandments" (Mat. xix. 17).

Moreover, we are bound to keep them, not merely in their bare literal sense, but with all the explanations and additions made by our Divine Redeemer.

In other words, we must understand them, as the Catholic Church understands them, for in morals as in faith the Church is our infallible guide.

The First Commandment.

Thou shalt not have strange gods before me, &c.

156. The First Commandment, taken literally, simply forbids us to worship false gods and idols.

But it therefore *implies* that we must worship the one true and living God; as it is written elsewhere, "The Lord thy God shalt thou adore, and Him only shalt thou serve" (Mat iv. 10).

This is the great principle, or prime moral truth, which is enunciated in the First Commandment.

And the way to worship God, as the Church of Christ teaches, is by acts of Faith, Hope, Charity, and Religion.

157. Acts of Faith, Hope, and Charity.— We are commanded by the First Commandment to live always in Faith, Hope, and Charity, and sometimes to make declaration before God, that we believe in all that He has taught, that we hope to possess Him in heaven, and that we love Him with all our heart.

We may do this either in a set form of words (as in the prayer-books), or by doing or saying anything, in which those acts are then and there expressed or implied, as by praying, hearing Mass, receiving the Sacraments; by crossing ourselves devoutly, taking holy water, or using any other sacramental; by genuflecting to the Blessed Sacrament, or bowing to a Crucifix.

We must make, as is clear, acts of Faith, Hope, and Charity in some form or other: (1) When we come to the use of reason, or at least to the knowledge of this obligation; (2) at the hour of our death; (3) whenever we are bound to hear Mass, or receive a Sacrament; (4) when tempted to sin, and (5) after sinning, against either of these virtues.

158. Confessing the Faith.—We are bound sometimes to acknowledge that we are Catholics, even at the risk of our lives.

This happens when God's honour or our neighbour's spiritual good requires it; for instance, whenever, through hatred of our holy religion, we are challenged by infidels or heretics.

For our Lord says, " He that shall be ashamed of Me *and of My words*, of him the Son of Man shall be ashamed, when He shall come in His majesty," &c. (Luke ix. 26).

It is not wrong, however, to hide our Faith, at least for a time, as did Joseph of Arimathea, who was " a disciple of Jesus, but secretly, for fear of the Jews " (John xix. 38), and Nicodemus, who " came to Him first by night " (*v.* 39); provided we simply conceal the fact that we are Catholics, without pretending by word or act to be anything else.

159. Religion.—All acts by which God is honoured are acts of Religion; and the virtue which inclines us to do such acts is the virtue of Religion.

The chief internal acts of Religion are Adoration and Prayer.

The chief external acts of Religion are Sacrifice, the other services of the Church, the reception of the Sacraments, keeping lawful oaths and vows, and the observance of the Sunday.

By these and such like acts we manifest our Faith, Hope, and Charity, our sense of the greatness, goodness, and supreme dominion of God, our utter dependence upon Him, our gratitude for past and hope of future favours, and our wish that all creatures may praise Him, bless Him and do His will, together with our sorrow for sin, and our endeavour to make satisfaction for it.

The act of Religion especially commanded by the First Commandment is Adoration.

160. Adoration is the payment of that high homage or worship which is due to God alone, as the Sovereign Lord of all things.

An act of Adoration, therefore, is any thought, word, or deed, by which we acknowledge that God is First, Best, and Greatest, and the High Lord and Master of all that is.

Adoration and Charity are not the same thing; yet an act of Adoration almost always contains an act of Charity.

To bless and praise God for being what He is, to rejoice in the Divine perfections, to thank Him "for His great Glory," and the like, are acts of Adoration.

The *Gloria*, which is sung in the Mass, the hymn, *Te Deum*, many of the Psalms and Hymns of the Church, are acts of Adoration.

By Adoration we increase the glory of God: not His essential or eternal glory, for that cannot be increased; but His accidental glory, which may be increased, and which God desires to have increased by our free acts.

161. The Worship of the Saints.—We cannot love God without loving whatever He loves; nor can we honour Him by refusing to honour those whom He has delighted to honour.

So, if we love God, we must honour His friends and servants, the Angels and the Saints.

We honour them, therefore, by thanking them for having served God so well; by singing their praises; by adorning their statues and pictures; by choosing them to be our Patrons; by asking their prayers, that we may serve God as well as they did; and most of all by imitating their virtues.

162. The Worship of Mary.—Of all creatures the nearest and dearest to God is the Blessed Virgin Mary.

She—after, of course, the Humanity of Christ—is the best, the purest, the most exalted of creatures. Of her alone "was born JESUS, who is called the Christ" (Mat. i. 16). To her, in a sense, we owe the Incarnation; for she *might have refused* to be "the handmaid of the Lord" (Luke i. 38), and the "Mother of Sorrows." And lastly, as God gave His Son through her, and in no other way, so doubtless he gives through her, and in no other way, many graces and blessings.

For all these reasons, she deserves our special love and worship.

163. Degrees of Worship.—It is clear that God alone may be worshipped *as God*, as the Master of life and death, as the Maker and Sovereign Lord of all. This worship is called by theologians *latría*.

The worship of the Saints, as the servants and special friends of God, is called *dulía*.

The worship of Mary, as being *above* what is due to other Saints, is called *hyperdulía*.

164. The Worship of Relics and Images. —Sacred Relics are things that have in some way belonged to our Blessed Lord or to the Saints.

Thus the Cross, and the Crown of Thorns, are relics of our Saviour; the relics of the Saints are their bodies, clothes, or other things that belonged to them.

In all times God has honoured His Saints by working miracles with their relics; for instance, with the mantle of Elias (4 Kings ii. 14), with the rod of Moses (Exod. vii.), and with the bones of Eliseus (4 Kings xiii. 21); with our Saviour's garment (Mat. ix. 20, 21; xiv. 36), with handkerchiefs and aprons which had touched the body of St. Paul (Acts xix. 12); nay, with the mere shadow of St. Peter (Acts v. 15, 16).

Sacred Images, for example, the cherubim of beaten gold (Exod. xxv. 8), and the brazen serpent (Numb. xxi. 8), were made by the command of God; and by means of these also He worked miracles.

Now, relics and images remind us of Christ and His sufferings, and of the Saints who have walked in His footsteps, and so they excite us to devotion.

And as we honour God by honouring His Saints, who are made by nature and grace to His image and likeness, so we honour both God and his Saints by honouring sacred relics and images.

But of course we never *pray* to relics or images, for they, being lifeless, can neither see, nor hear, nor help us.

There is, therefore, *all the difference* in the world between the right use of sacred images, and the sin of Idolatry, with which some anti-Catholic writers try to confound it.

165. Sins against the First Commandment.—All sins against Faith, Hope, Charity and Religion are sins against the First Commandment.

166. Sins against Faith:—

Atheism, or denying the existence of God.

Deism, or denying that God has ever revealed Himself.

Agnosticism, or denying that anything can be known about God or a future state.

Mahometanism, or following the false prophet Mahomet, instead of Christ.

Judaism, or following the Mosaic Law, denying that Jesus was the Messias, and saying that the Christ is yet to come.

Heresy, or contradicting the Church's teaching, and choosing one's own belief, whilst professing to be a Christian.

Remaining a Protestant, Jew, or Infidel, whilst knowing the truth of the Catholic Religion.

Denying or doubting any article of Faith.

Apostasy, or ceasing to believe, or to practise, the Religion of Christ.

Ignorance, if wilful, of the "Our Father," the "Hail Mary," the Creed, the substance of the Commandments of God and of the Church, the way to receive the Sacraments worthily, or the chief duties of one's state of life.

Endangering one's Faith by reading bad books or papers, by going with anti-Catholic companions, by marrying non-Catholics, or by listening to teachers and preachers of false religions.

Supporting false teachers, contributing to the funds of heretical churches or chapels, or Protestant Bible or Missionary Societies.

167. Sins against Hope :—

Presumption, or leading a life of sin, and depending on a late, or on a death-bed repentance; expecting to be saved without using the means of salvation.

Despair, or losing all hope of salvation; thinking one's self, like Cain, too wicked to be forgiven; persuading one's self it is no good trying any more to be good, as if God's grace were powerless, and God did not earnestly wish every sinner to be converted and saved.

Neglecting to pray: to say no prayers for a whole day, would be a venial sin; to say none for several weeks would probably be a mortal sin.

And lastly, wilful distraction in prayer.

168. Sins against Charity :—

Hatred of God, of our Lady, of the Saints, of Religion, or of anything as being consecrated to God.

Injuring our own or another's body or soul.

Causing others to sin.

Not sending for a priest when anyone is in danger of death.

In fact, all sins are sins against Charity, for mortal sin deprives the soul of Charity; and every venial sin is a step towards mortal sin.

169. Sins against Religion :—

Since God is the Sovereign Lord of all things, and must therefore be worshipped as such;

Since God has made known by what acts He will be worshipped, propitiated, and moved to bestow grace and salvation;

Since "every best gift and every perfect gift is *from above*, coming down from the Father of light" (James i. 17);

And since He has appointed the means by which all good things, like knowledge, health, and prosperity, are to be obtained—namely, (1) care and industry, and the proper use of the powers of nature, and (2) our own and the Church's prayers, by which all we do and have and use may be blessed and rendered more than naturally productive;

It follows that to seek knowledge, health, riches, or anything else by any other means than those which God has made lawful,—even to seek our salvation by any other acts than those of that Religion which He has revealed—is insulting to God's Providence, and therefore sinful.

So the following are sins against the First Commandment :—

Idolatry, or worshipping creatures, that is, men living or dead, angels or devils, animals, birds, trees, rivers, the sun, moon, and stars, or any "graven thing, or the likeness of any thing that is in the heaven above, or in the earth beneath, or in the waters under the earth," as if any such creature were a god.

Dealing with the devil: trying by his aid to get knowledge of future events, to find hidden things, to be cured or to cure other people of diseases, to get money, to be lucky, to gain any advantage, or what is worse, to do mischief to anyone, to make people hate each other, to excite them to carnal love, or any such like things.

Superstition, by which there is attributed to certain words, gestures, or material things a power which God has not given them, such as the power of warding off evil, or bringing good, or the power of foretelling things to come.

Using charms, spells, or incantations, for any purpose, good or bad.

Trusting to omens: believing that the course of the stars, the flight of birds, the lines of the hand, signs on the earth, dreams, the howling of dogs at night, the ticking of the death-watch, or the like, are certain signs of good or bad luck, of death, of future happiness or misery.

Consulting astrologers, fortune-tellers, witches, spiritualistic "mediums," &c.

Putting faith in dream-books, astrological almanacks, and the like.

Believing that some days are lucky, and some unlucky, on which to be married, to set out on a journey, to commence an undertaking, &c.

False Religion, which is a kind of superstition: believing it possible, for instance, to be saved by faith alone, or by reading the Bible, or by being of any religion or no religion, so long as one is honest.

Joining in the services of a false religion.

Pretending to be a Protestant or denying that one is a Catholic, through fear or shame or human respect, to escape danger, or for purposes of gain.

Tempting God, or asking Him to show His power, or to work a miracle without cause, as the devil wished Christ to do (Matt. iv. 5, 7).

Appealing to God (except in cases of special inspiration, or for special need) to prove one's innocence or to cure a disease by miracle.

Sacrilege, or profaning any person, place, or thing that is dedicated to God.

Simony, or the sin of Simon Magus (Acts. viii.), that is, buying or selling a sacred thing, like the priesthood, or a bishopric, or the cure of souls.

And, lastly, Pride and Sloth are sins against Religion.

The Second Commandment.

Thou shalt not take the name of the Lord thy God in vain.

170. We are commanded by this commandment to honour, and forbidden to dishonour, the name of God.

It is a duty of Religion to " praise the name of the Lord " (Ps. cxii. 1 ; cxlviii. 2) ; and our Saviour has taught us to pray—" Hallowed be Thy name."

171. We honour the name of God when we speak of Him piously, seriously and reverently, and the oftener we do this the better ; when we praise Him in psalms and hymns, and spiritual canticles ; when we ask God to bless us, to bless other people, to bless our food, or to bless other things that are useful to soul or body ; when we make a pious vow, or take a lawful oath ; and when we faithfully observe it.

172. Oaths and Vows.—To swear, or to take an oath, is to call God to witness, either that what we say is true, or that what we promise we intend and bind ourselves under pain of sin to perform.

An oath can lawfully be taken only after due deliberation, for some good and weighty purpose, when God's honour, our own or our neighbour's good, requires it : as before giving evidence in a court of justice, or in making some solemn compact.

A vow is a deliberate promise made to God, binding under pain of sin, to do some good thing for God's greater honour and glory.

A vow, or a promissory oath, binds, under pain of mortal sin, if the promise was to do an important matter, as to hear Mass, to fast, to keep a grave secret, or the like; but under venial sin only, if the matter of the promise was of little importance, or if, in the case of a vow, it was only intended to bind under venial sin.

So strict is the obligation before God of keeping lawful oaths and vows, that no one, as a rule, ought so to bind himself without much consideration, and the leave of a learned and prudent confessor. There are cases, however, in which vows become null and void, and cases in which the Church has power to dispense from their fulfilment, or to commute or change the good work vowed into some other, for good and weighty reasons.

173. Sins against the Second Commandment :—

Blasphemy, that is, saying or thinking anything injurious to the honour of God. Wilful blasphemy is a mortal sin. It is blasphemy to deny any of the Divine Perfections; to accuse God of falsehood, cruelty, or any other sin; to mock Him; to curse Him, or wish Him evil; to wish there was no God, or that He could not punish sin; to curse God's wind or rain; to revile the Blessed Virgin and the Saints, the Church, the Sacraments, the Holy Mass; to say that Holy Scripture is false or immoral in its teaching; or to say, write, print, or publish anything of similar import.

Perjury, or taking a false oath, that is, swearing what one believes to be false; or taking an oath to do something, with the intention of not performing it.

Rash oaths, or swearing without judgment, deliberation or knowledge of what one is doing.

Unjust oaths, or swearing to do wrong. To take a Fenian or Masonic oath, or to become with an oath a member of any secret society, is a mortal sin.

Unnecessary oaths, or swearing without grave reason or necessity.

Likewise, vowing to do wrong, or to do anything

unworthy of God (see Mal. i. 14 ; Deut. xxiii. 18).

Cursing, that is, wishing evil to oneself, to another, or to any of God's 'creatures; as that the devil may take them, that God may damn them, and the like.

It is also sinful, though seldom grievously so, to use God's name in joke, or as a sign of impatience or irritation.

And, lastly, it is a sin to break a vow or a promissory oath which has been lawfully and rightly made or taken : for such vow or oath is a law to the man that has made or taken it, and binds him like a law. But never, on the other hand, is it binding—never even is it lawful—to keep an unjust or unlawful oath or vow. For what it was a sin to vow, it must needs be a sin to do.

The amount of guilt in all these sins is in proportion to the injury which is wilfully done or intended to God, or to any of His creatures. For sometimes oaths and curses are uttered without thought, without malice, without knowledge of the meaning of the words, and therefore, at least to some extent, without sin.

THE THIRD COMMANDMENT.

Remember that thou keep holy the Sabbath Day.

174. The Old and New Sabbath.—From the beginning of the world, Saturday, the seventh day of the week, was observed as the Sabbath or day of rest and prayer, in memory of the creation, and, from the time of Moses, in memory of the deliverance of the Israelites from Egyptian bondage (Deut. v. 15).

But the Christian Church, from its very commencement, has kept instead the first day of the week, or Sunday, as the Lord's Day, in memory of our Lord's Resurrection and of the Descent of the Holy Ghost, both of which happened on the first day of the week.

To keep the Sunday holy we must do two things—rest from servile work, and be present at holy Mass.

175. The Sunday Rest.—We are bound, as a

rule, not to do any servile work or manual labour, such as digging, ploughing, weaving, sewing, building, and the like, during the whole of the Sunday, that is, from midnight to midnight.

Judges, lawyers, counsel, auctioneers, merchants, dealers, and shop-keepers are forbidden to do their public work, or transact business in their courts, shops, or markets, on the Lord's Day.

To do business or work of these kinds on the Sunday for any considerable time, say two or three hours, would be a grievous sin.

We are commanded to rest from work on the Sunday (1) that we may have time and opportunity for hearing Mass, going to the Sacraments, prayer, receiving instruction, and reading good books; and (2) that those who gain their bread by the sweat of their brow may obtain that rest for mind and body which they need at least once in seven days.

Sometimes, however, it is lawful to work on a Sunday, namely, (1) for such a purpose as to relieve the sick, to bury the dead, or to do any work which piety towards God or charity to our neighbour may render needful; (2) when those that do it are very poor, and obliged to earn every trifle they can; (3) in cases of necessity, when work must be done in order to avoid great loss from storm, fire, accident, or any other cause (see Luke xiv. 5); and (4) it is lawful to cook, dust, sweep the house, and do other light domestic work.

176. Occupations not Servile.—Such occupations as reading, writing, drawing, and the like, and all amusements, whether of mind or body, such as playing at chess, billiards, cricket, or tennis, running, jumping, and the like, are lawful on the Sunday, provided they do not interfere with the duties we owe to God; for such things have never been forbidden by any law of God or of the Church. It is becoming, however, to indulge in them on the Sunday with moderation and circumspection.

177. Hearing Mass.—This Commandment, as explained by the Church, bids us keep the Sunday holy by hearing Mass.

The Mass, as will be shown later on, is the great Christian Sacrifice, and the highest act of worship that man can pay to God.

We are, therefore, bound, under mortal sin, to be present every Sunday in some church, chapel, or other place where there is public Mass, during the time when Mass is celebrated.

We are also bound to assist at it, with attention and devotion, from the beginning to the end.

To hear only part of the Mass through our own neglect is sinful : and, indeed, grievously sinful, if the part we omit to attend be long, as from the beginning to the offertory, or if it include the Elevation, or probably if it include the Communion only.

To miss Mass, however, in whole or in part, through accident, or illness, or press of work which cannot be put off, or distance from Church, or when to hear it would cause great inconvenience to ourselves or others, is no sin.

The Fourth Commandment.

Honour thy Father and thy Mother.

178. This commandment, as understood in the Church, enforces the duty of obedience and respect to all lawful superiors.

For the father of the family was originally also the priest and the temporal ruler ; and, in fact, the same great reason exists for honouring the ecclesiastical or the civil ruler as for honouring a parent, namely, that, by God's dispensation, all lawful superiors in some way hold God's place and exercise His authority over us.

This commandment, therefore, regards the duties (1) of children to their parents, (2) of all other subjects to their superiors, and (3) of the duties of parents and superiors to all beneath them.

179. The Duties of Children to their Parents.—These are (1) to love them with filial piety, or a true, sincere, and inward affection; to wish them well; to pray for them; and to help them in their temporal needs.

(2) To pay them honour and respect in thought, word, and deed.

(3) To obey them in all that is not sin.

180. Hence Children Sin:—If they show their parents no signs of love, treat them harshly, or scowl upon them;

Much more if they hate them, curse them ("He that curseth his father or mother, dying, let him die," Lev. xx. 9); if they wish them dead, or wish any evil to befall them;

If they provoke them to anger, or cause them trouble, pain, or annoyance; much more if they make their parents sin;

If they do not assist them in poverty or affliction; and especially if they do not procure for them, in case of need, the means of receiving the last Sacrament;

If they strike their parents—a crime which God ordered to be punished with death (Exod. xxi. 15).

If they threaten them, treat them with contempt, or expose their sins or failings without grave and serious reason;

If, through pride, they despise their parents as poor and uneducated, or refuse to recognise them, or publicly ridicule them;

If, before they are men or women, and as long as they are under their parents' authority, they refuse to obey them, either in matters of morals, or of religion, or of household arrangements; for instance,—

If they go into company, or seek amusement, to which their parents object; or if, against their parents' will, they endanger their morals or their good name, by company-keeping, especially late at night, or at any unreasonable times or places;

If, against their parents' command, they neglect Mass, the Sacraments, or other religious duties ;

If at school, or during apprenticeship, they waste their time, and so put their parents or others to useless expense ;

If by disobedience to their parents' commands, they in any way endanger the good order or the peace of their families ;

And, generally, if they engage to be married without their parents' knowledge and consent.

With respect to sins of disobedience, however, three things must be observed—(1) that parents must not be obeyed if they command anything sinful ; (2) that they need not be obeyed if they command anything grossly unreasonable, as, for instance, if they command a child to marry where there is no affection, or not to marry where there is no reasonable ground of objection ; and (3) that in order to make disobedience a grave sin, there must be an unmistakeable command, and not merely persuasion or desire, on the part of the parent.

181. The Duties of Parents.—Parents are bound by the law of nature to love their children.

They are bound to take reasonable care, from the first moment of a child's existence, to preserve it from all danger of disease or death, and to provide it during infancy and youth with food, shelter and raiment, according to their means.

Parents are bound to send their children to school, or otherwise to give them a serviceable education, and somehow to provide them with the means of living honestly in the future.

Above all, they are bound to instruct their children, or to get them instructed, in the truths and practices of the Christian Religion ; to correct them of their faults, and sometimes, if need be, prudently and moderately to punish them (see Prov. xiii. 24 ; xxiii. 14 ; Eph. vi. 4) ; and to set them good example.

182. Hence Parents Sin :—If they hate their children, or curse them, or fail to help them in time of need;

If they call them evil names;

If they make known their children's faults, except to each other for mutual counsel;

If they spoil them by over-indulgence;

If, by favouring one above the others, they give occasion to quarrelling and discord;

If they in any way endanger the life of a child, even yet unborn, either through malice or through carelessness;

If they fail to give their children due support when young, or send them adrift upon the world before they are well able to provide for themselves;

If they knowingly expose them to danger from fire, water, animals, dangerous play-things, or amusements;

If they neglect to obtain and to follow medical advice for a child that is sick, or give it instead old women's nostrums;

If they keep their children away from school, bring them up in ignorance, teach them no trade or occupation by which they may gain in after life an honest living;

If they do not instruct them, or get them instructed, in their Religion;

If they give them no correction, when correction is needed, or, on the other hand, punish them too severely with danger to life or limb;

If they give them bad example by cursing, swearing, gambling, drinking, or using impure language in their presence;

If they allow them to neglect their religion, or to endanger their faith or morals by reading bad literature, keeping bad company, &c.;

And last, but not least, if they send their children to Board Schools, or entrust them to bad, irreligious, or anti-Catholic teachers. As a rule, when a Catholic School is at hand, it is a mortal sin to send a child to any other.

183. The Duties of Husband and Wife.— Married people are bound to love each other, and to live together.

The husband is bound, as the head of the family, to support, to guide, and to correct, when needful, the rest of the household.

The wife who, though "under the power of her husband" (Gen. iii. 16), is not his servant, but his consort, must honour and obey him, and serve him in household matters.

184. The Duty of other Relations.— Grand-parents and grand-children, brothers and sisters, and other relations, are not bound, indeed, so strictly as parents and children are bound, but yet are bound to have a love and care for each other, in proportion to their degree of relationship, more than for others who are "neighbours" and nothing more.

When anyone, indeed, is in very great poverty, his relatives, if able, are bound, under pain of sin, more than others, to give him help.

185. The Duties of other Superiors and their Subjects.—(1) The Pope, Bishops, and Priests are bound to teach truth, to exhort to virtue, to administer the Sacraments, to denounce scandals, to visit the sick, and to help the dying, even at the risk of their lives.

We are, therefore, bound to obey them in spiritual matters, to give them the honour which is due to their sacred character, and to contribute to their support.

All sins of calumny, detraction, public ridicule and the like, are much more grievous when committed against a priest, because of the injury which is thereby done to Religion and to the honour of God.

(2) Kings, Magistrates, and temporal Rulers are bound, under pain of sin, according to their place and power, to devote themselves to the public good, to defend their country, to maintain order, to protect the

weak, to administer justice impartially, to repress immorality, to punish injustice, theft, and violation of right, to respect the liberty of the subject in all well-doing, and, above all, to protect Religion.

They sin most grievously if they make bad laws against the rights of the Church, or the just liberties of the people; if they use their power for extortion or any unworthy end; or if they fail grievously in any of the above-named duties.

We are bound, on our part, to " be subject to higher powers" that "are ordained of God" (Rom. xiii. 1), to be faithful and loyal citizens, and to obey the just laws of the country in which we live.

To belong to a secret society, which plots against the State, is a mortal sin, and is punished by the Church with excommunication.

(3) Teachers and Guardians are delegates of the parents. They have, therefore, for the time being parental authority over their pupils and wards; and also parental responsibility.

The same reverence and obedience (though not the same inward affection) is due from a pupil to a teacher, as from a child to a parent. Contempt, stubbornness, and disobedience shown to a teacher, is, therefore, sin against the Fourth Commandment.

(4) Masters and mistresses are bound to see that their servants observe the law of God, and that they know the chief truths of faith.

They must give their servants time to fulfil their religious duties.

They must treat them with kindness, especially in time of illness, give them good advice, show them good example, and pay them their wages punctually.

Catholic people should always, if possible, have Catholic servants; and if they have servants who are not Catholics, they should pray for their conversion, lend them good books, and show them, by word and example, the divine truth and beauty of the Catholic Religion.

Servants sin if they neglect their work, waste the property of their employers, backbite or calumniate them, or reveal their family secrets.

Servants, like other people, are bound, at all risks, to keep the Ten Commandments; but they are not bound, for instance, to fast, to abstain from meat on Fridays, or to hear Mass on Sundays, if their doing so would cause great inconvenience to themselves or others, or be likely to lose them their places.

But servants, like others, are bound, at all risks, to keep the laws of the Church, whenever they are bidden, through contempt or hatred of the Faith, to break them; for to break, in such cases, the Church's laws, is to sin against faith and against religion.

Catholic servants should get, if they can, situations in Catholic families; and all servants sin if they remain in situations where their faith or morals are seriously endangered.

The Fifth Commandment.

Thou shalt not kill.

186. The Fifth Commandment supposes, and, therefore, implicitly enjoins, the love of ourselves and of our neighbours, and all that is involved therein.

As understood in the Church, this commandment forbids (1) all kinds of murder, or the wilful and unauthorised killing of any human being, man, woman, child, or unborn infant; (2) all injury to our own or our neighbour's body, which is the beginning of murder; (3) immoderate anger, hatred, and every evil will, which lead to murder; and (4) scandal and bad example, which are spiritual murder.

187. Murder or Bodily Injury.—Soldiers in battle, in a war which they believe to be just, may kill or wound the enemy without sin.

Public executioners punish or put to death, without sin, criminals condemned by lawful authority.

In self-defence, or in defence of an innocent person, any private person may lawfully strike or wound an unjust assailant; and may even, *if no other means of escape be available*, save his own life, or that of the innocent person unjustly attacked, by killing the unjust assailant.

But in all other cases wilfully to take the life of any human being, whether by shooting, stabbing, poisoning, or by any other means, is a most grievous crime, being one of those sins that are said to "cry to heaven for vengeance."

It is a mortal sin to commit suicide, or to kill one's own self, for any purpose, or by any means whatever.

It is also a grievous sin notably to shorten one's own or another's life, or to expose one's self or another to the danger of death: unless there be very grave reason, as, for instance, when a fireman risks his life to save the inmates of a burning house, or a soldier to defend his country, or a nurse in taking care of the sick.

Duelling, too, is a most grievous sin, and is punished by the Church with excommunication.

Moreover, it is sinful to fight, or to quarrel.

It is sinful to give way to immoderate anger, or to resentment in excess of what is due to an evil deed, whether done to ourselves or others.

It is sinful to bear hatred or malice, even to those who have really and wilfully injured us.

It is sinful to seek or to wish to be revenged, upon our enemies.

But it is not sinful to feel proportionate and moderate resentment at an evil deed, whether done to ourselves or to others, nor to shun the wicked on account of their sins, nor even to prosecute evil-doers, provided our motive be not revenge.

It is also a sin to eat or drink too much, because it injures health and shortens life.

Gluttony, if notable, and drunkenness are mortal sins.

And, lastly, contumely, threatening, calling names,

angry, injurious, and abusive words are forbidden by the Fifth Commandment, as partaking of the nature of bodily injury, and often leading to it.

188. Soul-Murder or Scandal.—Scandal is any word or deed which may lead or give occasion to another person to sin.

It is *direct* scandal to say or do anything sinful, or apparently sinful, with the intention of leading another into sin.

It is *indirect* scandal to do or say anything sinful, or apparently sinful, without such intention, but with the knowledge that it will, or may, be an occasion of sin to some other person.

We are guilty of scandal, and answerable, more or less, for the sins of others, if we set them bad example ; or advise or persuade them to sin ; or command them to sin ; or provoke them to sin ; or help them to sin ; or give them, sell them, or lend them, immodest or infidel books, papers, or pictures, or induce them to join in or be present at immodest plays, dances, or other amusements, and so put sin in their way ; or flatter them for their sin ; or hide them while sinning, and so give them opportunity to sin ; or defend their past sins ; or consent to the sins of our children, or those under our charge ; or remain silent when by speaking we might easily hinder any sin.

To give scandal is a dreadful sin ; for our Lord has said, "Woe to the world because of scandals," and "Woe to that man by whom the scandal cometh" (Matt. xviii. 7).

People sometimes, however, take scandal from the innocent words or actions of others, through their own weakness, ignorance, or foolishness ; this is called the scandal of the weak ; and we ought not to give it if we can easily avoid doing so.

And some, like the Pharisees of old, through their own wickedness and perversity, take scandal even at the best of actions ; this is called Pharisaical scandal, and no one, as a rule, is bound to guard against giving it.

THE SIXTH COMMANDMENT.

Thou shalt not commit adultery.

189. This commandment pre-supposes the Divine laws of marriage, namely, (1) that a man may have one wife, and a woman one husband only; and (2) that the contract of marriage can only be dissolved by the death of one of the parties.

It obliges all people to observe purity, according to their state of life ; and it forbids all contrary acts, which, done with deliberation, are mortal sins.

Moreover, it forbids whatever is contrary to modesty in thought, word, or deed.

It is sinful, therefore, to read immodest books or papers ; much more to write, print, lend, sell, or publish them ; to frequent bad theatres or music halls ; to sing bad songs ; to gaze at immodest objects, whether pictures, statues, or living things ; and to join in or listen, with pleasure, to wicked conversation.

In short, it is sinful in any way to seek impure gratification, or to do or think of anything, *without good and lawful reason*, which may be the occasion of it, even against our will.

190. God's Hatred of Impurity, or unchastity, is shown by those dreadful punishments with which He visited this sin on many occasions—by the fate of Sodom and Gomorrah (Gen. xviii., xix.; Jude v. 7) ; by the fate of the twenty-four thousand who had sinned with the daughters of Moab (Numb. xxv. 9) ; by the punishment of death which He decreed against the unchaste in many instances ; and by the numerous denunciations of all kinds of impurity throughout the Old and New Testaments.

" Fornicators and adulterers God will judge " (Heb. xiii. 4).

"Neither fornicators, nor idolaters, nor adulterers, nor the effeminate, nor liers with mankind . . . . shall possess the kingdom of God" (1 Cor. vi. 9, 10).

And St. Paul says,—"Fornication, and all uncleanness, or covetousness (evil desire), let it *not so much as be named amongst you,* as becometh saints" (Eph. v. 3).

The Seventh Commandment.

Thou shalt not steal.

191. This commandment forbids us to take or to keep unjustly whatever belongs to another, or to do wilful damage to another's goods or property.

It is, therefore, a sin to commit theft or larceny, that is, to take secretly what belongs to another.

It is a greater sin to rob with violence either to person or property, as by highway robbery, or burglary, that is, breaking into houses or offices in order to steal.

All kinds of cheating in buying and selling, using false weights or measures, passing bad money, selling as genuine adulterated food or damaged articles, and the like, are species of theft, and are forbidden by this commandment.

So also to damage or destroy the property of another without just and lawful reason, to waste an employer's time or property, to appropriate portions of material intended to be worked up, to injure a person's business by taking away his character, and such like acts, are so many forms of theft.

So also are oppression of the poor, and defrauding labourers of their wages—two sins which cry to heaven for vengeance.

It is also a sin for a judge to take a bribe to give either a just or an unjust sentence, for a lawyer or barrister by any means to cause unnecessary expense, for a witness to injure another by giving false testimony, and for anyone to engage in an unjust lawsuit.

And, lastly, it is a sin to take more interest for the loan of money than is warranted by the risk one runs in lending it and by the loss one incurs, or would ordinarily incur, by being deprived of the use of it during the time it is lent.

To take a fair and moderate interest is lawful ; to make use of a neighbour's misfortune to exact of him more than this, is the sin of usury, which is a kind of oppression of the poor.

It is also a sin against the Seventh Commandment to refuse or delay to pay our debts, to buy or receive stolen goods, to take no means to discover the owner and restore to him things we may have found, or not to make restitution, when restitution is due.

192. Restitution.—We are commanded not to keep that which belongs to another, without his consent.

In other words, we are commanded, whenever we are able, to pay our debts; to return what we have borrowed; to give back what we have stolen, or at least its value; and to make full compensation for injury we have wilfully done.

The duty of making restitution binds, under pain of mortal sin, where the injury done has been grave, and under pain of venial sin, where the injury has been but small.

But when numbers of small thefts have been committed, especially from the same person, until the injury done amounts to something serious, then the obligation of making restitution binds under pain of mortal sin.

193. The Amount of Sin in all cases of theft or damage is measured by the injury which is foreseen by the guilty party, at least as likely to be inflicted by his act upon the party robbed or injured.

If the injury is considerable, the sin is mortal; if the injury is slight, the sin is venial.

But since between mortal and venial sin, in the matter of theft, it is impossible to draw a certain line, therefore all injustice, however small, should be most carefully avoided.

The Eighth Commandment.

Thou shalt not bear false witness against thy neighbour.

194. The sins forbidden by this commandment are false testimony, lying, calumny, detraction, backbiting, injurious words, rash judgment, and, in short, all words or speeches or writing which injure our neighbour's character.

False testimony is telling a lie upon oath in a court of justice.

This is (1) a sin against truth, (2) a sin against the honour due to the name of God, being a false oath or perjury, and thus forbidden by the Second Commandment, and, (3) when it causes an injury to another person, a sin against justice, and thus forbidden by the Seventh Commandment.

False testimony, given upon oath, be its purpose ever so good, be it even to save an innocent man from death, is always a mortal sin.

A lie is to say what one knows or believes to be untrue, with the intention to deceive.

A lie which is told to do harm or injury is called a malicious lie, and is a mortal sin if the injury be great, and a venial sin if the injury be small.

Lies of excuse, lies told in jest, if there be any real deception in them, and all those little untruths that are sometimes called white lies, are sins; for God has said, " You shall not lie, neither shall any man deceive his neighbour " (Lev. xix. 11).

Where there is no deception, of course, there is no sin; so that writers of stories, and those that make puns and jokes, commit no sin against truth, since what they write and say is not intended to be taken seriously and believed.

Calumny or slander is to say or insinuate anything which we know or suspect to be false against our neighbour.

It is a sin against truth, charity, and justice, and is mortal, when the injury done is great.

Detraction is making known, without sufficient reason, the real but secret faults of our neighbour.

If this does a serious injury to our neighbour's character, it is a mortal sin.

We may lawfully, however, make known the sin of an evil-doer, (1) whenever his own good requires it, that is, we may tell it in charity to a superior, that the superior may instruct and correct him; (2) whenever this is necessary in order to remove suspicion from ourselves or any other innocent person; and (3) to prevent grave injury to the state, to the people at large, to religion, or to private persons.

Backbiting is a name we give in England to all sins of calumny, detraction, and uncharitable conversation, committed against an absent person.

Injurious words, such as reproaches, nasty insinuations, sarcasm, raillery, and all similar insults offered without very good reason, to a person's face, are sins against the Eighth Commandment, and are generally prompted by jealousy, hatred, or pride.

195. Restitution for Calumny and Detraction.

—He that has injured his neighbour by speaking ill of him must undo the mischief he has done, and restore the good name of his neighbour as far as he can.

He that has lied to the injury of his neighbour must contradict the lies that he has told; and where the injury done is great, and amounts to a mortal sin, he is bound, under pain of mortal sin, not only to contradict the falsehoods he has told, but also to make compensation to his injured neighbour to the extent of the injury done him.

He that has sinned against his neighbour by simple detraction, or saying, without just cause, what is true, indeed, but to his neighbour's discredit, must make satisfaction by showing him in public some kindness, or mark of respect, or by saying some good about his neighbour to counteract the evil.

Injury which is done by disrespect, injurious words, &c., may be repaired by acts and words of an opposite kind.

THE NINTH AND TENTH COMMANDMENTS.

Thou shalt not covet thy neighbour's house, neither shalt thou desire his wife, nor his servant, nor his handmaid, nor his ox, nor anything that is his.

196. This sentence has always been looked upon in the Church as containing two commandments. For, as it is easy to see, two distinct sins are forbidden by it. Our Blessed Lord has said, "Whosoever looketh on a woman to lust after her, hath already committed adultery with her in his heart" (Mat. v. 28). And this adultery of the heart is forbidden by the words, "Neither shalt thou desire his wife." But to covet, that is, to wish to obtain by unjust means, our neighbour's house, or cattle, or other goods, is a sin against the eternal law of justice, enunciated, not by the Sixth, but by the Seventh Commandment, "Thou shalt not steal."

These commandments are, therefore, usually quoted in the Church as follows :—

NINTH COMMANDMENT, "*Thou shalt not covet thy neighbour's wife.*"

TENTH COMMANDMENT, "*Thou shalt not covet thy neighbour's goods.*"*

And the Ninth is understood as forbidding all sins of thought against purity, and the Tenth as forbidding all sins of thought against justice.

---

* This is also the *order of the words* in the Septuagint.

197. Evil Thoughts.—" Evil thoughts," says the Scripture, "are an abomination to the Lord" (Prov. xv. 26). And again, " Perverse thoughts separate from God" (Wisd. i. 3).

It is possible, therefore, to sin by thought, and, moreover, to sin by thought with that mortal or killing sin which "separates" the soul "from God."

When a thought comes first into the mind to do an impure or unjust act, it is only a temptation, and not a sin.

No matter how frequently a bad thought enters, or how long it stays in the mind, if it enter and stay against the will, it is still only a temptation, and not a sin.

Moreover, we can think of a sinful action as a matter of history, or as a mere supposition, and reason about its causes, and its consequences; and this is not a sin.

But it *is* a sin to make sinful thoughts our own; to take wilful delight or pleasure in the idea of saying or doing a wicked thing; to take wilful delight or pleasure in a bad deed done by ourselves or by others; to consent or agree with them that do evil (Rom. i. 32), and to think how pleasant it would be to do the same; or to be sorry for having done right, or for not having done some sinful deed.

In short, it is a sin to think of anything evil, *with a wilful affection towards it*.

Much worse a sin is it to wish, or desire, or to form the intention, to do some wicked deed. This is the sin precisely forbidden by the Ninth and Tenth Commandments.

The wish or intention in any way to sin against holy purity is a mortal sin.

The wish or intention to offend God in any other way is mortal or venial, according as the deed, if done, would be mortal or venial.

In all cases the wish or intent to do evil is a sin of the very same kind and malice as the act that is wished or intended.

198. Temptations.—The angel said to Tobias, "*Because* thou wast *acceptable* to God, it was *necessary* that temptation should prove thee" (Tob. xii. 13).

And St. James says, "*Blessed* is the man that endureth temptation; for when he hath been proved, he shall receive the crown of life, which God hath promised to them that love Him" (i. 12).

Have we temptations? If so, it is a sign that, like Tobias, and like St. Paul, we are "acceptable to God." Do we resist them? If we do, we are "blessed." God "Himself tempteth no man" (James i. 13), but he allows our own concupiscence to entice us to sin, that having been "proved" we may "receive the crown."

199. How to conquer Temptation.—Pray to God earnestly, frequently, and *specially* for the grace to resist your particular temptation.

Ask the Blessed Virgin, your Guardian Angel, and the Saints to help you.

Go frequently to the Sacraments.

Mortify yourself, according to circumstance, by fasting, abstinence, and temperance.

Be modest at all times and places, for modesty is the guardian virtue of chastity.

In time of temptation, remember—death and judgment are nigh at hand, and then—heaven or hell for ever.

Avoid all occasions of sin, namely, persons, places, books, amusements, or hours of ease and idleness, which are known from sad experience to be dangerous.

Live in the presence of God, and in the "fear of the Lord," which "is the beginning of wisdom."

Be distrustful indeed of yourself, but have great confidence in God.

And lastly, be always resolved, by the grace of God, never to yield to temptation, nor to risk the loss of heaven, nor to "crucify again to yourself the Son of God, making Him a mockery" (Heb. vi. 6).

CHAPTER VI.
THE SEVEN SACRAMENTS.

200. The Sacraments are Baptism, Confirmation, the Holy Eucharist, Penance, Extreme Unction, Holy Order, and Matrimony.

The Sacraments are signs of grace.

Each Sacrament was instituted by our Lord Jesus Christ, to convey sanctifying grace to our souls; and each conveys it for some particular purpose peculiar to itself.

And each of them indicates in some way what purpose it is for which its grace is given.

They are, therefore, outward signs of inward grace, and signs, moreover, which actually convey the grace they signify.

BAPTISM.

201. Baptism is the first of the Sacraments, and the most necessary for salvation.

Our Lord said to Nicodemus, "Unless a man be born again of water, and the Holy Ghost, he cannot enter into the kingdom of God" (John iii. 5).

Our Lord's last charge to His apostles was—"Go ye, therefore, teach all nations, *baptising* them in the name of the Father, and of the Son, and of the Holy Ghost" (Mat. xxviii. 19).

And He added, "He that believeth and *is baptised* shall be saved, but he that believeth not shall be condemned" (Mark xvi. 16).

On the day of Pentecost St. Peter said to the wondering crowd, "Repent, and *be baptised* every one of you, in the name of Jesus Christ, for the remission of your sins" (Acts ii. 38).

And St. Paul, after his miraculous conversion, and after doing penance for three days, was told to "arise and *be baptised*, and wash away [his] sins" (Acts xxii. 16).

202. Infant Baptism.—There was some doubt among Christians whether infants ought or ought not to be baptised.

Holy Scripture says nothing about infant baptism.

But St. Irenæus in the second century, says: "All are saved who are regenerated in Christ; infants, youths, and aged men" (Ad. Hær. lib. ii. 39).

Origen says: "The Church hath received a tradition from the Apostles to give baptism also to little ones" (Lib. v. in cap. 6 ad Rom.).

Many other Fathers bear witness to the same tradition.

And the Church, in fact, has long since decided that Baptism can and must be given to infants.

Curiously enough, most Protestant sects practise Infant Baptism, as the Catholic Church does, on the strength of Tradition, and in spite of their boast that "the Bible only is the Religion of Protestants."

203. The Minister of Baptism.—A Bishop or priest is the ordinary minister of Baptism.

But in case of necessity, when a child is dying, and a priest is not to be found, anybody may baptise it.

A Catholic, however, should do it rather than a Protestant; a man rather than a woman; another person rather than the father or mother; but, above all, one that knows how to do it, even though it be the father or mother, rather than one that does not.

Whoever baptises another becomes a spiritual relative of the baptised and of the parents of the baptised, and this relationship is a diriment impediment to matrimony.

So that a boy, for instance, who baptised a little girl in danger of death, could afterwards marry neither her nor her mother.

And a girl who baptised a boy could afterwards marry neither him nor his father.

204. How Baptism is given.—The minister, whether a priest or any other person, takes *common water;*

He pours it on the face of the child, or on the skin of its head;

And whilst he is pouring it, he says: "*I baptise thee in the name of the Father, and of the Son, and of the Holy Ghost.*"

This is all that is necessary for a real, true Baptism, to make a child a Christian, and to give it a right to enter heaven.

205. Solemn Baptism is Baptism administered by a bishop or priest (or by a deacon, with the bishop's leave), in the Church, with many holy ceremonies and exorcisms, and with water that has been solemnly blessed for this purpose, and consecrated with the holy oils.

As the rite of Solemn Baptism is given in most large Prayer Books, it will suffice to say here:—

(1) That children ought, as a rule, to be brought to the Church on the first or second Sunday after they are born, to be solemnly baptised.

(2) That if, through danger of death, a child has been privately baptised at home, it must, if it recover, be brought to the Church that the ceremonies may be supplied, that a name may be given it, and that its name may be entered in the Baptismal Register.

And (3) that when a child is sent to be solemnly baptised, one sponsor at least, or one of each sex at most, a godfather and a godmother, must be provided for it.

206. The Sponsors, or the Godfather and Godmother should be good Catholics. No unbeliever, heretic, excommunicate, public criminal, person of bad character, or of unsound mind, is allowed by the Church to be godfather or godmother.

The Church also objects to persons that have not been confirmed, and much more to persons that are "out of the Church," through having omitted their Easter Communion.

The sponsors must be appointed by the parents, or by the parish priest; they must intend to undertake the responsibilities of their relationship with their godchild; and they must, at the very moment of the baptism, either by themselves, or by a proxy, touch the child.

A fitting person, duly appointed, but unable to be present, may stand sponsor by proxy; another person answering and touching the child by his authorisation.

The sponsors undertake, in any default of the parents, to instruct their godchild in Christian faith and morals.

The sponsors also, like the minister of Baptism, contract a spiritual relationship, *not* indeed *with each other*, but with the child and its parents;

So that marriage is impossible between a godfather and his goddaughter or her mother; and between a a godmother and her godson, or his father.

Before bringing the child to the Church the sponsors should make sure that they know—

(1) The name or names to be given to the child; one of which at least must be that of a Saint, and none may be of evil meaning, or of bad repute;

(2) The names in full of the child's father and mother, and the mother's maiden name;

(3) The date of the child's birth;

And (4) whether it has been baptised at home, and if so, by whom and how.

207. The Dispositions for Baptism.—The adult recipient of Baptism must have—

(1) Faith, and some knowledge at least, of the Christian Religion;

(2) The intention of receiving the Sacrament;

(3) Sorrow for his actual sins;
(4) The resolve to lead a Christian life.

All this is involved in the promises which are made before Baptism, either by the person to be baptised, or by his godfather or godmother for him.

These promises are—" To renounce Satan, and all his works and pomps."

In other words, he must give up all affection to every kind of mortal sin; for otherwise he would not be justified, but would commit a sin of sacrilege, by receiving this Sacrament.

A child, however, not old enough to use his reason, cannot have any affection to mortal sin, and is, therefore, justified by the power of the Sacrament, having nothing in his soul to hinder its effects.

208. The Effects of Baptism.—The effects which the Holy Ghost produces in the soul by means of Baptism rightly received are these:—

He blots out original sin.

He blots out all mortal sins which the recipient has previously committed.

He blots out all venial sins previously committed, for which the recipient is sorry; but not those for which he retains an affection.

He cancels *all* the punishment due for the sins remitted.

He gives the soul sanctifying grace.

And with sanctifying grace He infuses the virtues or habits of Faith, Hope, Charity, and all those other virtues which are modes or varieties (so to speak) of Charity; or, in other words, He gives to the baptised an abiding and supernatural disposition to observe the baptismal promise to "renounce the devil, and all his works and pomps," and to keep God's law; and, as abiding aids to this end, He bestows the "Seven Gifts of the Spirit."

He likewise impresses upon the soul an indelible mark or character.

This mark or character makes the baptised a child of God in a new and supernatural sense; whence Baptism is called a *re-generation* or *new birth*.

It makes him a Christian, that is, a member of Christ and of His mystical body, the Church;

It gives him a right and capacity to receive other Sacraments, and to receive certain actual graces in time of need;

And it makes him an heir, a co-heir with Christ, to the kingdom of heaven.

Thus the act of baptising, which signifies a washing or cleansing, effects what it signifies, namely, the cleansing of the soul from the stain of sin.

Note.—When Baptism is received by an adult who retains an affection for some mortal sin that he has committed, he receives indeed the baptismal character, but not the forgiveness of his sins, nor sanctifying grace, nor the infused virtues, nor the gifts of the Holy Ghost.

To gain all these, he must seek justification, either by the actual reception of the Sacrament of Penance, or by an act of perfect charity or contrition with the wish and intent to go to confession as soon as he can.

209. The Necessity of Baptism.—Baptism is the most necessary of the Sacraments.

No unbaptised person can be a member of the Church.

No person that dies, through his own fault, unbaptised, can enter heaven.

Therefore, grown up people, as yet unbaptised, are bound, under pain of mortal sin, to receive this Sacrament as soon as they conveniently can, after they know the obligation.

And parents are bound, as a rule, under pain of mortal sin, to send their children to Church to be baptised within a week or two after birth; or to get them baptised at home, by a priest if possible, in case of danger of death.

Note.—Of the fate of infants that die unbaptised, or of adults that die unbaptised, who, through lack of knowledge and understanding, are, all their lives, to all intents and purposes, infants, nothing whatever has been revealed to us. But that they do not enter heaven is certain, and that they do not suffer any positive punishment is almost as certain. Their eternal abode is probably that limbo, or "borderland," on the outskirts of heaven, in a state of natural happiness, where the souls of the righteous that died before Christ were detained until His coming.

210. The Baptism of Desire, and the Baptism of Blood.—In cases where actual Baptism is impossible, there are two means of justification, which, because they are in some sense substitutes for the Baptism of Water and of the Holy Ghost, are called the Baptism of Desire and the Baptism of Blood.

The Baptism of Desire (or of Fire, as it is sometimes called) is simply an act of pure love of God, or an act of perfect contrition, made by one not yet baptised.

Such an act of charity or contrition necessarily includes a desire of Baptism, if the unbaptised has knowledge of Baptism.

And whether or not, it includes a virtual desire of Baptism, in the general wish and intent to do God's will in *all* things.

It is, therefore, called the Baptism of Desire.

The Baptism of Desire brings sanctifying grace and the remission of original and actual sin.

But the Baptism of Desire is not a Sacrament.

It does not necessarily effect, as the Baptism of Water does, the remission of all temporal punishment due to past mortal sins.

It does not give the baptismal character.

And therefore it does not exempt from the grave and urgent obligation of receiving Sacramental Baptism, given the knowledge and opportunity.

The Baptism of Blood is martyrdom suffered by one not yet baptised.

To suffer martyrdom is to allow one's self to be put to death rather than offend God by denying any article of faith, or by sinning against any Christian virtue.

In infants, as for instance in the case of the Holy Innocents, death suffered from a tyrant through his hatred of Christ is accounted martyrdom.

When martyrdom is suffered, as it sometimes has been, before Baptism, it has a kind of sacramental effect.

It does not indeed give the sacramental character;

But if there be in the martyr any love of God, and at least that kind of sorrow for sin, called attrition, which springs chiefly from fear of God's eternal punishment, the Baptism of Blood is held to justify him, and to free him from all stain of sin and all temporal punishment due to it, and to obtain his immediate admission into the kingdom of heaven.

This is clear from the Church's unvarying practice from the very beginning, *never* to pray *for* the martyrs, but always to pray *to* them.

211. Heretical Baptism.—There is only one Lord, one Faith, and one Baptism (Eph. iv. 5).

And therefore, if a child is really baptised, even by a Protestant or other heretical minister, it receives the Baptism of Christ, and is made a member, not of the English Establishment, or of any other sect, but of the one true Church of Christ.

So far, then, the child is a Catholic, and not a Protestant, and "the Church of its Baptism" is the Church of Rome, the only Church of God.

It may, after that, be brought up in the errors of Protestantism, but should it, in time to come, by the grace of God, submit to the Catholic Church, it will then, in fact, be *rejoining*, not leaving, "the Church of its Baptism."

212. Conditional Baptism.—To baptise conditionally is to say, "*If thou art alive*, I baptise thee," &c.; or, "*If thou art not baptised*, I baptise thee," &c.

The first form is used when the minister of Baptism is in doubt whether the human being before him is living or not; and the second, whenever there is doubt whether a person has been really baptised.

Converts from Protestantism are always conditionally baptised, unless it is known for certain that they have been baptised in the proper way before.

213. The Reception of Converts.—Jews, and others who are certainly unbaptised, are received into the Church by unconditional Baptism simply.

But those that have been christened in some Protestant church or chapel are received as follows:—

(1) *After a course of instruction* they present themselves at some appointed time to a priest, at the altar.

(2) The priest recites some prayers, in which the convert mentally joins.

(3) The convert reads a profession of Faith.*

(4) The convert is absolved from any censures incurred by his heresy and schism. During this the convert will do well to say the "Confiteor," and to make an act of contrition.

(5) The priest baptises the convert, saying, "*If thou art not baptised*, I baptise thee, in the name of the Father, and of the Son, and of the Holy Ghost."

---

*The following has been sanctioned for this purpose:—
"I (N. or M.) do sincerely and solemnly declare that, having been brought up in the Protestant *(or other)* religion, but now, by the grace of God, having been brought to the knowledge of the Truth, I firmly believe and profess all that the Holy Catholic and Roman Church believes and teaches, and I reject and condemn all that she rejects and condemns."

But this shorter form should not be used if the convert can read the Creed of Pope Pius IV. For all these matters, at greater length, see "Catholic Belief," by the Very Rev. Joseph Faà di Bruno, D.D. (Burns and Oates.)

(6) After this the convert makes a general confession of the sins of his life, and is conditionally absolved.

So that, if the convert has never been really baptised before, his sins, unless remitted by a previous act of contrition, are now forgiven by Baptism; if he *has* been baptised in time past, the present conditional Baptism is null and void, and his sins are forgiven by the sacramental absolution (see Sacrament of Penance).

Confirmation.

214. Confirmation is the second of the Sacraments, and is, as it were, the completion of Baptism.

The word Confirmation means a *strengthening*.

This Sacrament is so called because it strengthens the Faith which is given in Baptism, and gives to those that receive it worthily grace and courage to profess their Faith, especially in times of danger and persecution.

And this strengthening is effected by a special infusion of the Holy Ghost.

For we read in Scripture that "when the Apostles, who were in Jerusalem, had heard that Samaria had received the word of God, they sent unto them Peter and John, who, when they were come, prayed for them, that they might receive the Holy Ghost, for He was not as yet come upon any of them: but they were only baptised in the name of the Lord Jesus; then they laid their hands upon them, and they received the Holy Ghost" (Acts viii. 14—17.)

From which passage, as well as from the constant practice and teaching of the Church, it is clear:—

(1) That Baptism and Confirmation are distinct Sacraments;

(2) That deacons, like Philip, could not confer the Sacrament of Confirmation, but only the Apostles, or the Bishops of the Church;

(3) That prayer, and the laying on of hands, were the means by which the Holy Ghost was given.

And that the imposition of hands was accompanied

by an unction, or anointing, is clear from St. Paul's words (2 Cor. i. 21), "Now He that confirmeth us with you in Christ, and that hath *anointed* us, is God; who also hath sealed us, and given the pledge of the Spirit in our hearts."

215. The Minister of Confirmation.— The *ordinary* minister of Confirmation is a Bishop only.

But the Pope may appoint a Priest as an *extraordinary* minister for a place where a Bishop could seldom or never be found.

216. How Confirmation is given.—The Bishop prays that the Holy Ghost may come down upon the person, or persons, to be confirmed;

He lays his hand upon the head of each one of them;

He makes the sign of the cross with chrism on the forehead of each;

At the same time saying these words: "I sign thee with the sign of the cross, and I confirm thee with the chrism of salvation, in the name of the Father, and of the Son, and of the Holy Ghost. Amen."

Then the Bishop gives the person confirmed a little blow on the cheek, saying, "Peace be with you," to teach him to bear meekly and patiently all crosses and persecutions, for the love and imitation of Christ our Lord.

The chrism is olive oil mixed with balm of Gilead; the oil signifying strength, and the balm the sweet odour of sanctity.

It is solemnly blessed or consecrated by a Bishop on Maundy Thursday.

217. Dispositions for Confirmation.—To receive Confirmation worthily, the recipient must be (1) baptised, and (2) in the state of grace, or free from mortal sin; "for Wisdom will not enter into a malicious soul, nor dwell in a body subject to sins" (Wisd. i. 4).

The Church also nowadays requires that the recipient have a knowledge, at least, of the chief mysteries of Faith.

Therefore children are usually confirmed at the age of eight or ten years; though in early times this Sacrament was conferred upon infants immediately after Baptism.

And, lastly, like the Apostles, who "continued with one accord in prayer, with the women, and Mary, the mother of Jesus, and with His brethren" (Acts i. 14), awaiting the Holy Ghost, the recipient should previously spend some time in prayer; for God the Father will "give the good Spirit *to them that ask Him*" (Luke xi. 13).

218. The Effects of Confirmation.—In this Sacrament the Holy Ghost takes possession of the soul.

He increases the sanctifying grace and charity previously received: for "the charity of God is poured forth in our hearts by the Holy Ghost, Who is given to us (Rom. v. 5).

He becomes to each soul, in a certain measure, as He is to the Church in full, "the Spirit of Truth" (John xvi. 13)—God the Illuminator.

He becomes by Confirmation, in a special sense, our Paraclete, Advocate, or Comforter; "for we know not what we should pray for as we ought, but the Spirit Himself asketh for us with unspeakable groanings" (Rom. viii. 26).

He becomes to us in a special sense, as He is called by Isaias, "the Spirit of Wisdom and of Understanding, the Spirit of Counsel and of Fortitude, the Spirit of Knowledge and of Godliness, and the Spirit of the Fear of the Lord" (Isaias xi. 2).

And His fruit in our souls, if we only act up to His grace and follow His promptings, is "Charity, Joy, Peace, Patience, Kindness, Goodness, Longanimity, Mildness, Faithfulness, Modesty, Continence, Chastity" (Gal. v. 22).

He likewise imprints upon the soul a mark or character, similar to that of Baptism, which can never be blotted out, not even by the fire of hell.

As the character of Baptism makes us once and for ever Christians and children of God, though we may afterwards lose all the benefit of that character by sin, so the character of Confirmation makes us once and for ever, to our greater glory in heaven or greater pain in hell, soldiers of Jesus Christ.

Great, then, are the graces, and great is the dignity conferred in Confirmation; and in order to preserve these graces and dignity, the confirmed will do well to read the exhortation of St. Paul to the Ephesians (iv. v. vi.), wherein he says, "Grieve not the Holy Spirit of God, in whom you are sealed unto the day of redemption."

219. The Need of Confirmation.—That men, as a rule, need Confirmation, and are, therefore, bound, under pain of mortal sin, some time in their life, when they have the opportunity, to receive this Sacrament, is clear from the very act of its institution, and from the common traditional teaching and practice of the Church.

To neglect to receive this Sacrament through sloth or contempt, especially in one subject to temptations against faith, or to persecution, would, therefore, be a grave sin.

Nevertheless, Confirmation is not absolutely necessary for salvation, since, in fact, it was not instituted, like Baptism and Penance, to justify the sinner, but to increase the grace and holiness of those already justified.

220. Sponsors.—Every boy or man confirmed must have one godfather, and every girl or woman one godmother, who contracts precisely the same relationship and obligations as the sponsors in Baptism.

And the relationship contracted in Confirmation is

a diriment impediment to marriage between the sponsor and the parent of the one confirmed.

221. The Confirmation Name.—The person confirmed takes a new name, in addition to those of his Baptism.

This name must be that of a Saint, whom he chooses for his patron, and whose virtuous example in following Christ he resolves to strive to imitate.

The Holy Eucharist.

222. The Holy Eucharist is the Body and Blood of Jesus Christ, with His Soul and His Divinity, under the appearances of bread and wine.

The Eucharist is the holiest, the most venerable, and the most wonderful of all the Sacraments.

In the Eucharist our Blessed Lord's Sacred Humanity is both a Sacrament and a Sacrifice.

As a Sacrifice, it is offered up to God the Father at the moment of the consecration in the Mass, and as a Sacrament it is given to the faithful in Holy Communion.

The word *Eucharist* means "thanksgiving." This Sacrament is called the Holy Eucharist, (1) because our Saviour solemnly "gave thanks" when instituting it (Mat. xxvi. 27; 1 Cor. xi. 24); (2) because one of its chief effects is to excite us to gratitude towards God; and (3) because it is an offering worthy to be made to God in adequate thanksgiving for all His favours.

223. The Holy Eucharist Promised (John vi.).—One day our Lord miraculously fed 5,000 men with five loaves and two fishes.

The next day he said to them—"Labour not for the meat that perisheth, but for that which endureth unto everlasting life, *which the Son of Man will give you*" (*v.* 27).

Then he taught, in many words, the necessity of Faith, concluding thus—"Amen, Amen, I say unto you: He that believeth in Me hath everlasting life" (*v.* 47).

After which He promised the Holy Eucharist in these words:—" I am the living bread which came down from heaven. If any man eat of this bread, he shall live for ever: and the bread which I will give is My flesh, for the life of the world" (*vv.* 51, 52).

Then, in answer to the objection, "How can this Man give us His flesh to eat?" He said, "Amen, Amen (or *verily, verily*, words which He used when uttering solemnly the most important truths), I say unto you: Unless you eat the flesh of the Son of Man, and drink His blood, you shall not have life in you."

"He that eateth My flesh and drinketh My blood hath everlasting life: and I will raise him up in the last day" (*vv.* 53, 54, 55).

And, again, "He that eateth My flesh, and drinketh My blood, abideth in Me, and I in Him" (*v.* 57).

"As the living Father hath sent me, and I live by the Father, so he that *eateth* ME, the same also shall live by Me" (*v.* 58).

"This is the bread that came down from heaven. Not as your fathers did eat manna, and died. He that eateth this bread shall live for ever" (*v.* 59).

Then many of His disciples, like the Protestants of to-day, said: " This saying is hard, and who can hear it?" (*v.* 61). And they "went back, and walked no more with Him" (*v.* 67).

" Then Jesus said to the twelve: Will you also go away? And Simon Peter answered Him (and all Catholics answer with him), Lord, to whom shall we go? Thou hast the words of eternal life" (*v.* 69).

224. The Promise Fulfilled. The Institution of the Holy Eucharist (Mat. xxvi. 26—28; Mark xiv. 22—24; Luke xxii. 19—20; 1 Cor. xi. 23—25).

Our Lord, at His last supper, first fulfilled the law by eating the paschal lamb.

Then He took the chalice, and divided the wine among them (Luke xxii. 14—18).

After which He took bread, blessed it, broke it, gave thanks, and told His disciples to eat it, "For," He said, "THIS IS MY BODY;" St. Luke adds, "*which is given for you*," and St. Paul, "*which shall be delivered for you.*"

Then taking the chalice, or cup, and giving thanks, and telling them all to drink of it, which they did, He said (according to St. Matthew): "THIS IS MY BLOOD OF THE NEW TESTAMENT, *which shall be shed for many unto the remission of sins;*" or (according to St. Luke), "THIS CHALICE IS THE NEW TESTAMENT IN MY BLOOD, *which is (or shall be) shed for you.*"

These words we Catholics take in their true and natural sense, (1) because we believe, with St. Peter, that He who spoke them had "the words of eternal life" (John vi. 69); (2) because when they were spoken, the time was come when He spoke plainly, and no longer in parables (John xvi. 29); and (3), because if the words, "*This is My Body, This is My Blood,*" were meant to denote but a commemorative resemblance between bread and wine and the Body and Blood of Christ, they would be the most misleading words ever uttered; whereas, taken in their natural sense, they contain a last will and testament worthy of our dear Lord's boundless power and love.

225. Transubstantiation.—What our Lord took into His hands was bread;

But when He gave it to His disciples He said it was His Body.

Similarly, what was in the chalice was wine, according to Tradition;

But when He gave it them to drink He said it was His Blood.

So a change had been instantaneously made of the whole substance of the bread into the Body of Christ, and of the whole substance of the wine into His Blood.

This change is called Transubstantiation.

Any bread that we eat, or wine that we drink, suffers a kind of Transubstantiation, being partly changed, by a natural process, into our living body and blood.

But the change of bread and wine at the Last Supper into the Body and Blood of Christ was a complete and absolute change of substance, an instantaneous and miraculous Transubstantiation.

226. The Command to Consecrate.—St. Luke and St. Paul tell us that after our Lord had changed the bread into His Body, and given it to the disciples, He added, "Do this for a commemoration *(or* in remembrance) of Me."

And St. Paul tells us that, after He had changed the wine into His Blood, He said, "This do ye, as often as you shall drink it, for the commemoration *(or* in remembrance) of Me."

The pastors of the Church were thus commanded, and of course at the same time empowered (for the command would have been useless without the power) to do what Christ had done, namely, (1) by saying the words which He said, to change bread and wine into His Body and Blood, and (2) to distribute the Holy Eucharist to the faithful.

227. The Real Presence.—By the words of consecration, as they are called,—"This is My Body, This is My Blood," uttered by one having authority from Christ, Transubstantiation is effected.

By them the bread is *wholly* changed into the Body, and the wine into the Blood of Christ; though the colour, size, shape, taste, and other appearances (*species*, or *accidents*) of the bread and wine remain.

But because the Body of Christ is a living Body now, as it was at His Last Supper, it does not exist alone, under the appearance of bread; but there are also present His Precious Blood and His Soul, together with His Divinity, which never, for one moment, from the time of the Incarnation, has been separated either from His Body, or from His Blood, or from His Soul.

So also, although by force of the words there is present in the Eucharist, under the appearance of wine, only His Blood; yet, because living blood must be in a living body, our Lord's Body and Soul, together with His Divinity, are also present under the appearance of wine.

So under either species, and in every consecrated *host* or particle, and in every part of each, our Lord Jesus Christ is really present, whole and entire, as God and as Man.

Yet His Body is one and the same everywhere, though present at once in many thousands of places.

Our Blessed Lord's Soul in the Eucharist has all its natural faculties, as memory, understanding, will, the power of loving, &c.; and all its supernatural gifts and qualities, as the light of glory, the beatific vision, charity, and the gifts of the Holy Ghost.

And His Body in the Eucharist has all its various organs, limbs, and members, is permeated by the Precious Blood, and bears upon it the marks of His five most sacred wounds.

Yet our Lord does not use in the Eucharist any of His senses.

He does not see with His bodily eyes, nor hear with His ears, nor feel what is done to the species.

In all these matters He is, as it were, dead—"A lamb standing as it were slain" (Apoc. v. 6).

228. The Eucharist a Sacrifice.—For a Sacrifice there are needed:—

(1) A something to be offered to God, which, if living, is called a victim.

(2) A priest appointed by God to offer it;

(3) A sacrificial act, in which the victim or offering is slain, or destroyed, or otherwise changed to a state

of imperfection, and offered to God chiefly to adore Him as the Lord of life and death.

In the first offering of the Eucharistic Sacrifice, on the first Maundy Thursday, Christ's own living Body was the victim; Christ Himself was the priest; and He rendered Himself, beneath the forms of bread and wine, motionless, helpless, as if He were dead, already "slain, as it were," and reduced to the state of food.

And now that this sacrifice is offered by the ministry of men, still Christ's living Body is the victim; Christ is the principal Priest, giving power and effect to the words and acts of His ministers; and the sacrificial act is still the same—Christ mystically slain, and rendered motionless, helpless, as if he were dead, made into the form of meat and drink.

229. The Eucharist the Fulfilment of Prophecy.—Several prophecies are fulfilled in the Holy Eucharist, but two especially must here be noticed.

1. "The Lord hath sworn and He will not repent: Thou art a Priest for ever according to the order of Melchisedech" (Ps. cix. 4).

That these are words of prophecy applying to Christ and His priesthood is clear from St. Paul's quotation of them (Heb. v. 6, 10; vi. 20; and vii. *passim*), to prove the superiority of the priesthood of Christ over that of Aaron.

Now Melchisedech offered a sacrifice of bread and wine (Gen. xiv. 18). Christ, therefore, is a Priest of the order of Melchisedech, because He offered Himself in the form of bread and wine: and a priest *for ever* of that order, because by the ministry of men He offers Himself daily, and will offer Himself daily, upon our altars, in the form of bread and wine, until the end of the world.

2. "I have no pleasure in you (the Jewish priests) saith the Lord of Hosts: and I will not receive a gift from your hand; for from the rising of the sun, even

to the going down, My name is great among the Gentiles : and in every place there is sacrifice, and there is offered to my name a clean oblation" (Mal. i. 10).

These words are a *prophecy* : for when they were uttered the Jewish priesthood was not yet rejected, nor was God's name great among the Gentiles, nor was there *anywhere* among them a clean oblation made to Him.

These words are not a prophecy of the Sacrifice of the Cross ; for that was offered, not "in every place," nor "among the Gentiles," but in one place only, and among the Jews.

But they clearly apply to the Holy Eucharist.

For (1) the Jews have long since ceased to have a priesthood and a sacrifice.

(2) God's name is great, through the preaching of His Church, among the Gentiles ;

(3) In every place, or in every country of the world, there is the Eucharistic Sacrifice ;

(4) This is clearly a "clean oblation," being the Body and Blood of the Son of God, "the Lamb unspotted and undefiled" (1 Peter i. 19).

230. The Holy Sacrifice of the Mass.—That great and solemn act of worship in which Christ is daily offered as a clean oblation to His Father, under the forms of bread and wine, by the ministry of His priests, is called the HOLY MASS.

The Holy Mass begins with a psalm, a public confession of sins, made first by the priest and then by the people, with prayers for each other's pardon, and prayers that the priest may duly perform the great act of Sacrifice.

Then follow the offertory, or the blessing and the offering of the bread and wine, which are to be "consecrated," or changed into the Body and Blood of Christ, some secret prayers, and the Preface, or Festival Thanksgiving, ending in a song of joy, the *Sanctus* and *Benedictus*.

After this comes the Canon, consisting (1) of a prayer that the offerings there present may be accepted both for the Church at large, and for certain persons for whom the priest desires specially to pray; (2) of the CONSECRATION, in which our adorable Saviour becomes bodily present under the forms of the bread and the wine; (3) of an offering to the Eternal Father of our Blessed Lord's Body and Blood, in obedience to His command, in remembrance of His Passion, Resurrection, and Ascension, to obtain blessings for those that thall partake of this holy food; and (4) of prayers for the dead and for the living.

Then come prayers in preparation for Communion; and, lastly, the Holy Communion itself, in which the Body and Blood of Christ are partaken of by the priest, and by such of the faithful as desire to receive.

This concludes the Sacrifice, after which the people are dismissed with a blessing, and the opening words of the Gospel of St. John are read as an act of praise and thanksgiving.

231. The Altar and the Cross.—The Sacrifice of the Mass is no other than the Sacrifice of the Cross repeated day by day.

The Victim in both these Sacrifices is the Body and Blood of Jesus Christ.

The Priest in both is Christ Himself.

And both have the same four objects, namely, (1) to worship God as the Master of life and death and Sovereign Lord of all things; (2) to thank Him worthily for all His goodness; (3) to obtain the grace of repentance for all that are in sin, and the remission of temporal punishment for all that need it, whether living or dead; and (4) to beg other graces and blessings for soul and body, both for all men in general, and for some in particular.

On the following points, however, they differ:—

(1) Christ on the Cross shed His Blood in reality; but on the Altar He sheds it only mystically, and the

real separation of His Blood from His Body, which took place on the Cross, is signified by the separate consecration of bread and wine.

(2) On the Cross He offered Himself visibly; but on the altar He offers Himself invisibly.

(3) On the Cross He suffered pain and agony; in the consecration on the altar He suffers nothing, for "death shall no more have dominion over Him" (Rom. vi. 9).

(4) On the Cross He paid once and for all the price of our redemption, or actually merited for us justification and innumerable graces; on the Altar He does not merit these things again, but He offers, time after time, in our behalf, that death with its merits which He once and for all suffered on the Cross.

In short, He applies to us in the Mass the merits which He gained for us on the Cross.

(5) On the Cross He really died; on the Altar He is only dead, *as it were*, "standing *as if* slain."

And, lastly, our Lord, living, and yet as it were dead, upon the Altar, is a divine and perpetual commemoration of Himself who lived and died in human form.

232. To whom the Mass is offered.—The Holy Mass is offered to God alone.

For God alone is worthy to be worshipped by the sacrifice of so great a Victim.

But after the high worship paid in Mass to God alone, a secondary honour may be paid to God's chosen servants and special friends, the Saints and Angels, by commemorating their holiness, by thanking God for it, and for giving us their example, and by asking Him to hear their prayers in our behalf.

Masses in which this is done are called Masses of our Lady, of the Saints, or of the Angels, as the case may be.

233. By whom it is offered.—1 The Chief Offerer is Christ Himself.

I

In every Mass Christ offers, as Man, to the Blessed Trinity, His own Body and Blood, with all the merits of His passion and death.

This he does, (1) by working the miracle of Transubstantiation, in which the Sacrifice consists, and (2) by concurring in the sacrificial words and acts of the priest, His minister.

2. The priest also truly offers the holy Sacrifice.

For it is by the mouth of the priest that Christ says the words, "This is My Body; This is a cup of My Blood," by which Christ is made again a Sacrifice, being reduced to the state of meat and drink.

3. As Christ and His priests offer Mass for all the faithful, our Lord in His sacramental state belongs in some degree to each one of us.

Whenever, therefore, a Mass is said, every Christian may offer the Divine Victim therein present up to God. Each one may offer it to discharge his own personal debt of adoration; to give God thanks as well for His own great glory as for all that He has done for any of His creatures; to compensate the majesty of God for the injury done Him by sin; and in supplication for every grace and favour that the soul of man can lawfully desire.

234. The Fruits of the Holy Mass.—

In the Mass, as we have seen, God is worshipped for His sovereign goodness, and thanked for His infinite mercy.

He is moved, on the other hand—(1) to grant the grace of repentance to some, and the remission of temporal punishment to others, according to their needs; and (2) to bestow other graces, spiritual and temporal, upon such as are disposed by their faith, hope, charity, fervour, and spiritual needs to receive them.

These latter effects are called the Fruits of Holy Mass, and their object is to make us holier—freer from sin, and more full of hope and charity.

Some part of these fruits, or benefits, of Holy Mass must of course always go to the priest that celebrates the Mass, and to those that offer it with him, by " serving " it, hearing it, defraying the expenses, or by giving alms to have it offered for their intention.

Some other fruit, or benefit, of Holy Mass, can be applied at the will of the offerer, especially of the priest, to any other person, living or dead, so far as that person needs and is disposed to receive it.

And some other fruit, or benefit, from every Mass, accrues to the Church at large, both on earth and in purgatory.

Moreover, when Mass is offered as a special prayer for the suffering souls in purgatory, God certainly, in His mercy, hears that prayer, and, through the satisfactions of Christ, shortens their punishment.

235. How to hear Mass.—At Mass we should always remember that we are there, with Christ and His priest,—

To adore the Blessed Trinity ;

To thank Him for innumerable favours ;

To beg pardon for our own and others' sins ;

And to beg of Him all that we need for soul and body.

Our will and intention being to do this, it matters but little what form of prayer we use.

We may follow the priest in the words of the Missal ; we may use any of the various " Devotions for Mass ;" or we may read the " Jesus Psalter," or the Litany of the Holy Name, repeating each invocation that expresses our needs or excites our devotion.

We may pray during Mass chiefly for the souls in purgatory, or for the Church at large, or for the conversion of sinners, or for the perseverance of the good ; for friends, relatives, superiors, benefactors, enemies ; for every human soul, in fact, which is neither in heaven, beyond the need, nor in hell, beyond the reach, of God's mercy.

And we may ask for each and all every spiritual good whatever, and every temporal good that would not be at the same time a spiritual evil.

And, lastly, if we have "proved" ourselves and prepared our souls, we may receive our Lord in Holy Communion.

236. Holy Communion.—Our Lord has given us the privilege of uniting ourselves to Him, by receiving His Body and Blood in the form of food.

And lest, through a sense of unworthiness, we might not dare to avail ourselves of so great a privilege, He has given us also a command to eat His flesh and drink His blood (John vi. 54).

This eating His flesh and drinking His blood, under the appearance of bread, or of bread and wine, is called Communion.

And hence the Blessed Eucharist, thus given as a Sacrament to the faithful, is called the Holy Communion.

237. Communion in one kind.—Our Lord has commanded His priests to consecrate bread and wine, and to complete the Sacrifice by receiving the Blessed Sacrament under both forms.

This is to signify the separation of His Blood from His Body, and so to "show forth the death of the Lord until He come" (1 Cor. xi. 26).

But He left no directions for the laity, whether to receive under one or both forms.

The Church, however, has long since ordered, for good and wise reasons, that no one, whether priest or layman, except the priest who is actually celebrating the Mass, shall receive under the form of wine.

Protestants who object that the Church thus gives to the laity only a "mutilated Sacrament," are unmindful of this truth, that Christ is wholly present under either species; that as bread or as wine Christ is wholly received; and that, therefore, the celebrant at the altar who consumes both forms receives but the same whole undivided Christ as the communicant at the altar-rail who receives under one form only.

To receive under either form alone is, therefore, *both* to eat the flesh *and* to drink the Blood of the Son of Man (John vi. 54).

This also agrees with 1 Cor. xi. 27 : " Whosoever shall eat this bread, OR drink the chalice of the Lord unworthily, shall be guilty of the body AND of the blood of the Lord."

Note.—This text is corrupted in the Protestant Bible by the changing of OR into AND.

238. Dispositions for Communion.—To receive Communion worthily, that is, in such a manner as to please our blessed Lord, three things are required : (1) that we be in the state of grace, or free from the guilt of mortal sin ; (2) that we be fasting from midnight ; and (3) that we spend some time previously in acts of devotion, and some time afterwards in acts of thanksgiving.

(1) The State of Grace.—" Let a man prove himself : and so let him eat of that bread, and drink of the chalice, for he that eateth and drinketh unworthily eateth and drinketh judgment to himself, not discerning the body of the Lord " (1 Cor. xi. 28, 29).

To receive Communion, therefore, knowingly and wilfully, in mortal sin, would be another mortal sin of sacrilege.

Therefore, every one conscious of having committed a mortal sin since his last confession is bound to go to confession, and to obtain absolution before receiving the Holy Communion.

As a rule, however, all Christians confess even venial sins before going to Communion, so that they may receive the more worthily.

(2) The Sacramental Fast.—Out of reverence to our Blessed Lord, we are forbidden by the Church to swallow anything, however small, in the shape of food or drink before Communion.

In other words, we are bound strictly to fast on the day of our Communion from the midnight until after we have received; so that if even by accident we eat so much as a crumb of bread, we must put off our Communion till another time.

It does not break the fast, however, to swallow blood from the gums, or to swallow *by accident* a small drop of water that may mingle with the saliva when we wash our teeth, or a fly, or dust, or bits of food that have adhered to the teeth from the night before, for to swallow such things is not eating or drinking properly so called.

(3) Acts of Devotion proper for before and after Communion are given in the Prayer Books.

In point of time, the preparation should begin, at the very least, half an hour before the moment of receiving.

And acts of thanksgiving, prayer, and praise should always immediately follow our Communion for the space at least of a quarter of an hour; for about so long does our Lord remain *sacramentally* with us.

It should also be added that we ought to approach the Holy Table clean, becomingly dressed, and with great gravity and reverence.

The more particular directions as to the manner of assisting at Mass, and receiving the Holy Eucharist, must be sought from a priest or well-instructed Catholic.

239. How often to Receive.—It is hardly prudent for any one who desires to live in the grace of God to receive Communion less frequently than once a month.

But such as avoid, as a rule, all mortal sin, and are striving to avoid even venial sins and imperfections, and to lead a more perfect life, may communicate once a fortnight, once a week, or even oftener, according to their needs and dispositions and opportunities, and accordingly to the advice of their confessor.

240. The Effects of Holy Communion.

—" If any man eat of this bread he shall live for ever : and the bread that I will give is My flesh for the life of the world (John vi. 52).

" He that eateth My flesh and drinketh My blood, hath everlasting life : and I will raise him up in the last day " (vi. 55).

" He that eateth My flesh, and drinketh My blood, abideth in Me, and I in him " (vi. 57).

" He that eateth Me, the same also shall live by Me " (vi. 58).

" He that eateth this bread shall live for ever " (vi. 59).

In Holy Communion, therefore, we receive (1) an increase of sanctifying grace and love of God, (2) innumerable actual graces, (3) the forgiveness of venial sins, (4) a remedy against temptation, (5) a cure for evil inclinations and (6) a pledge of everlasting life.

In Holy Communion we are united to Jesus by a sacramental union which lasts indeed for not many minutes, but with a spiritual union which lasts for ever, unless we dissolve it by committing a mortal sin.

241. Spiritual Communion.

—A Spiritual Communion is an earnest desire of receiving the Blessed Sacrament, when we have not the means to communicate in reality.

It may well be made at any time, but best in time of Mass.

To communicate spiritually, first (if in mortal sin make an act of contrition, and then) make an act of faith in Christ's real presence in the Blessed Sacrament.

Next imagine yourself communicating.

Then earnestly desire to receive our Lord sacramentally, and to be united with Him for ever.

Make other acts of hope, love, humility, &c., as at Sacramental Communion ;

And, lastly, acts of gratitude and thanksgiving.

This devotion has been earnestly recommended to the faithful by the Council of Trent.

242. Holy Viaticum.—When given to a dying person the Blessed Sacrament is called Viaticum, or the sacred provision for the journey of death.

The dying are bound, under pain of mortal sin, to receive the Holy Viaticum.

They may receive it fasting or not fasting.

As soon as a person is taken ill, before there are any signs of death, he should send, or his friends should send, to tell the priest.

And when the priest comes with the Holy Viaticum there should be prepared for him in the sick man's room—

A *table*, covered with a clean white cloth;

A *crucifix* and *two wax candles* on the table;

And an empty *cup* or wine glass, and some *clean cold water* in a jug.

When our Lord in the Blessed Sacrament enters a house, the inmates should receive Him on their knees; all noise should cease; and those who can should join in the prayers for the sick person's soul.

PENANCE.

243. The Sacrament of Penance is the ordinary means by which those that have sinned after their Baptism are forgiven and justified.

Our Lord Jesus Christ once wrought a miracle to prove that, as man, He had " power on earth to forgive sins " (Mat. ix. 6).

And the people that saw it were convinced, and " glorified God who gave such power to men " (Mat. ix. 8).

On the day of His Resurrection He said to His Apostles, " As the Father hath sent me, I also send you " (John xx. 21) : that is, He sent them, as men like Himself, with power to forgive sins; for St. John continues :—

"And as He said this He breathed on them, and said to them: Receive ye the Holy Ghost: whose sins you shall forgive, they are forgiven them; and whose sins you shall retain they are retained" (John xx. 22, 23).

God, therefore, has given to the pastors of His Church a judgment of souls in the matter of sins, with power to forgive such as repent, and to refuse forgiveness to such as refuse to repent.

244. What it is to Repent.—To repent is to acknowledge that sin is an evil, and that we have sinned;

To be displeased with ourselves for having committed it;

To hate and detest the evil that we have done;

To wish that we had not done it;

To resolve never to do it again;

To determine to make satisfaction, or undo the mischief we have done both to God and to men, as far as we can;

And, lastly, in us Christians, to repent is to seek God's forgiveness, or intend to seek it as soon as we can, by the only safe and easy means which God has given us, namely, the Sacrament of Penance.

And the Sacrament of Penance consists of the priest's Absolution, combined with Contrition, Confession, and Satisfaction.

245. Contrition.—Contrition is repentance, or sorrow for sin, with a resolve to sin no more.

The resolve to sin no more is called a "purpose of amendment," and invariably accompanies real sorrow.

Now, when we grieve for our sins, and make up our minds to leave off sinning, and take to serving God, we may do so for reasons of two distinct kinds.

(1) We may grieve to think that by sin we have robbed God's infinite goodness and majesty of some of His due honour and glory; that we have injured His loving-kindness, having "grieved the Spirit;" that we

caused our dear Saviour some portion of His agony and torments: and accordingly we may make up our minds to turn away from sin and live for God, *in order that* GOD *may be the gainer* by it; that we may make Him compensation for the injuries we have done Him; that we may give Him what is due to Him from every creature, eternal love and worship, thanks and praise; that, as far as we can help it, the Precious Blood shall not have been shed in vain. Repentance founded on such like motives is perfect Contrition, proceeding, as is clear, from goodwill and love towards God.

Or (2) we may have a practical sorrow for sin, and resolve to leave off sinning, and beg God to pardon us, *in order that* WE *may be the gainers by it;* that we may not suffer the punishment our sins have deserved, whether hell or purgatory; that our conscience may have peace, and we may live in hope; that we may do deeds of merit in the state of grace in the hope of heavenly rewards; that at last we may pass our eternity in happiness, and not in misery, since one or other it must be. Repentance of this kind—proceeding from mingled fear and hope—is called Attrition, or imperfect Contrition. By such repentance we seek our own well-being, and then turn to God as the only means of securing it.

Both these kinds of repentance are good.

Perfect Contrition, with a wish to receive the Sacrament, will in a moment justify any sinful soul.

And imperfect Contrition or Attrition, only, which is also a true and real repentance, disposes the soul for pardon and justification, *when the Sacrament is actually received.*

246. The Qualities of True Repentance.

—In short, true repentance, whether Contrition or Attrition, must be (1) *real, internal, and genuine,* not feigned, (2) *supernatural* in its motive, (3) *universal,* for all our mortal sins without exception, and (4) *supreme,* or paramount.

(1) We must repent, with a real internal sorrow of the will, not a sorrow of the feelings merely, or an outward sorrow feigned to deceive our confessor. There is no command to *feel* sorry, but only to *be* sorry. And real internal sorrow is known by our consciousness that we will and determine to avoid sin in the future.

(2) We must repent with some reference to God and our own salvation, that is, with either Contrition or Attrition, as explained above. This is what theologians mean when they say that our sorrow must come from a supernatural motive. For repentance without hope of pardon or purpose of amendment—remorse of conscience or vain regrets on account of pain, sickness, loss, reproaches, infamy, caused by sin,—is worse than useless in the sight of God. To regret without hoping and striving for pardon and amendment is not contrition but despair.

(3) We must repent of ALL our mortal sins, both those that we remember, and those that we do not, and resolve not to commit one of them again. For since the guilt of any one mortal sin separates the soul from God, the guilt of all must be forgiven, or the guilt of none. For sins are forgiven by the infusion of sanctifying grace; if, therefore, there be one mortal sin unrepented of, grace cannot enter the soul, and no sin can be forgiven.

(4) We must look upon sin as more to be avoided than all other evils, so as to be resolved never to commit another mortal sin for any pleasure or gain or love or fear of anything whatsoever.

247. Repentance for Venial Sins only.—

After mortal sin, venial sin is the greatest of evils.

Our repentance for venial sins ought, therefore, to be as real, and to spring from the same motives, as our repentance for mortal sin.

And though, of course, we ought to repent of *all* our venial sins, yet since affection for venial sin, unlike the affection for mortal sin, may exist in the soul together with sanctifying grace, some venial sins can be forgiven without the others.

Such, therefore, are forgiven as are repented of.

248. Confession.—Sacramental Confession is the telling of sins to a priest in order to obtain absolution.

Confession is as old as the time of Moses (see Num. v. 7).

The people confessed their sins to St. John the Baptist (Mark i. 5).

In the early Church, confession was often made in public, not always, as now, in secret.

So St. James says, "Confess your sins to one another, and pray for one another that you may be saved" (v. 16).

And St. John says, "If we say we have no sin, we deceive ourselves, and the truth is not in us. If we confess our sins, He is *faithful and just* to forgive us our sins" (1 John i. 9).

Now what makes Him faithful and just when He forgives the sins of them that confess to His priests is this, that He has made a promise,—"whose sins you shall forgive they are forgiven them" (John xx. 23).

So the Church has always taught what the Scriptures imply, that the priest has power from Christ to absolve, as a rule, those only who first confess their sins.

249. What Sins to Confess.—We are commanded to seek pardon for every mortal sin by means of the Sacrament of Penance.

Priests and Bishops, and the Pope himself, are bound by this rule as well as the laity.

We are, therefore, bound when we go to confession to confess every mortal sin that we have committed since our Baptism, except such as have been both confessed and forgiven in former confessions.

We must also tell the number of times, as nearly as we can, that each has been committed.

Of course sins forgotten cannot be confessed. God forgives them with the others, however, if we repent of *all*.

But mortal sins forgotten in former confessions must be confessed in the first confession at which we remember them; we are not, however, bound to go to confession on purpose to confess them before receiving Communion.

Together with the sins themselves, we must also confess anything about them that changes the nature of their guilt; thus, if anyone has robbed a Church, he must accuse himself of sacrilege as well as theft; or if any one has hated his parent, husband, wife, or other very near relative, this too must be confessed, for the sin is different from, and greater than, ordinary hatred.

It is also well to confess sins of doubtful guilt, mortal or venial, we know not which.

In short, it is well to confess all sins, great and small, and to repent of even the smallest offences against the goodness of God, that we may live in perfect charity.

250. When Sins must, or may, be confessed again.—(1) If ever we knowingly leave out a mortal sin in confession, or if we receive absolution whilst knowing, that for some particular mortal sin, or sins, we have no sorrow or purpose of amendment, we make a bad confession.

In a bad confession no sins are forgiven, but another sin, a mortal sin of sacrilege, is added to the former ones.

To be then restored to grace, we must confess both the sacrilege of the bad confession and all our other mortal sins that have not been rightly confessed in some former good confession.

To make a bad confession is a dreadful evil. Far better is it not to confess at all. For when one bad confession is made, it is generally followed by many others, and by many sacrilegious communions. From which may God deliver us.

(2) Another and far happier reason for telling old sins, is, that, when we go to confession very frequently, we may sometimes commit no sin of importance between one confession and another. It is then needful, if we wish to be absolved and to obtain the other graces of the Sacrament, to confess some sin of our past life; for unless some sin be confessed absolution cannot be given.

(3) And sometimes there is reason to make what is called a *General Confession;* that is, to confess all the sins of a year, of several years, or of all our life, though our previous confessions have all been good.

A General Confession is advisable when it is likely to increase our devotion, to make us realise our true spiritual state, to diminish our scruples, or to contribute in any other way to our spiritual good.

A General Confession should only be made on rare occasions, as in preparation for First Communion, or Marriage, or Holy Orders, or the taking of religious vows, or Extreme Unction, or in time of mission or retreat, and then with the consent of a prudent confessor.

251. The Utility of Confession.—In the institution of Confession our Lord Jesus Christ has shown His infinite wisdom.

For, surely, as a means to an end, confession, as practised in the Catholic Church, is the most calculated of all conceivable outward acts to detach the soul from sin, to turn it towards God, and so to dispose it for justification.

Confession is an act of humility, and, therefore, itself an almost certain act of true repentance.

The very act of confessing is an act of penance, and, therefore, in some measure, satisfies God for sin.

Confession makes the soul ashamed of sin, and the thought of it tends to deter us from sinning.

On the other hand, we are brought at confession close to Jesus, who is there in the person of His priest as a loving *Father,* welcoming back, consoling, forgiving, a penitent child.

We receive at confession instruction, counsel, guidance, and exhortations, suited to our own particular needs. We are told what means to take, and what penance to perform, in order to atone for the past, and to conquer temptation in the future. For the priest is there in the place of Christ, the *Physician* and *Teacher* of souls.

And, lastly, confession is not merely useful, but even necessary, in order that the priest, as judge in the place of Christ, may pass just judgment, by absolving those, and forgiving their sins, who are seen to be truly penitent, and of refusing absolution to such as will not give up sin, nor make needful restitution.

In short, God alone knows what evils are remedied, what losses made good, what injuries pardoned, what ill-gotten goods restored, what plots defeated, what scandals averted, what murders, revenge, and suicides prevented, by the grace of the Holy Spirit working through the medium of confession.

252. The Seal or Secrecy of Confession.—The priest who hears a Sacramental Confession is bound, both by charity, justice, the natural sanctity of a secret, the implied command of Christ, and by the express law of the Church, never to reveal—neither by word, nor sign, nor gesture; for no possible reason; to procure no good, to avert no evil; not under pain of death; neither during the lifetime, nor after the death of the penitent—without the penitent's express consent, either any of the sins confessed, or anything confessed about them, or in explanation of them, or the names or sins of accomplices, or the penance imposed.

And the priest may not even speak to the penitent himself about these things after he has left the confessional, unless it be for some good reason, and during confession, should the penitent confess to him again.

Likewise, all who by chance or wickedness overhear what is said by the priest or penitent during confession, are bound under pain of mortal sin never to make it known.

253. How to prepare for Confession.—
The preparation for confession is very simple: it consists in praying for grace, counting up our sins and truly repenting of them.

(1) We must pray to God for His grace to help us.

For this end we may say *Paters* and *Aves*, or pray in words of our own, or use the prayers in the prayer-books.

(2) We must carefully, at least for some few minutes, *examine our conscience*, or count the number of our different sins as accurately as we can.

Aids for examining our conscience are given in the prayer-books.

For one who has not lately confessed, it will be advisable to use some longer form by which the possible sins against each of the Commandments, against the duties of our various callings, and against the chief virtues of a Christian life, are suggested as aids to the memory.

For one who confesses frequently a much shorter form will suffice; or even, without using any form at all, a pious soul will easily recall its faults and failings.

(3) We must excite ourselves to repentance.

We may think awhile on the four last things— *Death*, soon, perhaps suddenly, to come upon us; *Judgment*, righteous and irrevocable, immediately to follow; and then which will it be, *Heaven* or *Hell?* That depends, perhaps, on this very confession.

Or we may think of the goodness of God, which our sins have outraged; of the sufferings of Christ which our sins caused; of the enormity of sin when viewed in the light of faith; or of any other truth of revelation which may excite in us sorrow and detestation of sin, and make us resolve to sin no more.

And then we must show, as it were, this our state of mind to our merciful God, and ask him to forgive us, or, in other words, make an act of contrition.

We may make it as follows, in the form of

254. A Prayer for Pardon.—Forgive me, Sweet Jesus, all my sins.

Forgive me; I will not sin again.

Forgive me, and be not angry with me for ever.

Forgive me, and punish me not in Thy dreadful fire.

Forgive me, and let me come to Thee.

Forgive me, and let not Thy Blood have been shed for me in vain.

Forgive me, and I will do Thy holy will.

Forgive me, and let me love Thee and praise Thee for ever.

255. How to make a Confession.—(1) Kneeling, make the sign of the Cross, and say—" In the name of the Father, and of the Son, and of the Holy Ghost. Amen." "Bless me, Father, for I have sinned;" "I confess to Almighty God," &c.

(2) Say how long it is since your last confession. Then tell your sins, your own and no one else's, except in so far as you have caused another person to sin. Tell them all, humbly, modestly, simply, in the fewest words possible, solely to obtain God's pardon.

(3) At the end say, "For these and all my other sins, which I cannot at present call to my remembrance, I am heartily sorry, purpose amendment for the future, and most humbly ask pardon of God, and penance and absolution of you, my ghostly Father." "Therefore I beseech," &c., to the end of the "Confiteor."

(4) Listen to the priest's instruction, if he gives you one, and to the penance he imposes.

(5) Then bow down your head, and renew your act of contrition, while the priest gives you absolution.

256. Satisfaction, or the Sacramental Penance.—Before the priest gives us absolution, or immediately after, he gives us a penance to perform.

A penance is always some act of prayer, fasting, or alms-deeds, or of some other kind of mortification.

In olden times long public penances were imposed for public sins. But now, short penances, in some way, however, proportionate to the sins confessed, are almost invariably substituted.

Sacramental penance is imposed (1) to make amends to the offended majesty of God, by inflicting punishment on the offending creature, and (2) to cure, as by a potent medicine, the wounds and weaknesses left on the soul by sin.

257. The Value of Sacramental Penance.—The Sacramental Penance, like all other acts of mortification, satisfies God for sin.

It restores to Him glory which sin deprived Him of; that is, not His eternal, essential, glory, which can neither be increased nor diminished, but that so-called "accidental" glory, which depends on the free worship of His creatures.

For penance being a punishment for sin, inflicted on ourselves, of our own free will, God accepts it instead of that temporal punishment, or some of it, at least, which is due for sin, and which must otherwise be endured in full in the flames of purgatory.

But because the Sacramental Penance *is* a part of the Sacrament, it is, therefore, more closely united with the merits of the Precious Blood of Christ.

And therefore any prayer or good work, when said or done as a Sacramental Penance, makes more satisfaction for sin than the same when said or done through private devotion.

And, therefore, lastly, the more Sacramental Penance is imposed upon us, even for venial sins, the better it is for us (if we are sure to perform it).

258. Performing the Penance.—As the confessor is strictly obliged to impose a penance, the penitent is obliged to accept it, to promise to perform it, and to perform it at the stated time, or as soon as he conveniently can.

To neglect to perform our penance, either altogether, or for a long time, say some months, would be a sin.

It would be a mortal sin if the penance was given for mortal sin; otherwise, a venial sin only.

If anyone forgets what the penance was, of course he cannot perform it, and then the omission is no sin; but he should go back and ask the confessor, if he can.

If a penance is given which we cannot easily perform, we should tell the priest, and ask him to give us another.

259. Absolution.—The priest's absolution is given in these words:—"I ABSOLVE THEE (that is, the penitent who has just confessed) FROM THY SINS, in the name of the Father, and of the Son, and of the Holy Ghost. Amen."

As sin is an offence against God, God alone can forgive it; God alone can remit the punishment due to it; God alone can restore a sinful soul to grace.

And this being so, it follows that the power of binding and loosing, the power of forgiving sins, does not belong to every man, but only to the Twelve Apostles to whom Christ Jesus gave it, and to those who have lawfully succeeded to their power and office, the Bishops and priests of the Church.

Moreover, as absolution is the exercise of judicial authority, no priest can validly absolve, unless he is either the spiritual superior over the person absolved, or a delegate of that superior.

Now the Pope is the spiritual superior, having spiritual jurisdiction, and the power of absolving, over all the world; for the power of binding and loosing, given in common to all the Apostles, was given in particular to St. Peter (Mat. xvi. 19).

The Bishops have similar jurisdiction, with some restrictions, throughout their dioceses, and parish priests in their parishes.

Other priests can validly absolve, only when approved and appointed to hear confessions, either by the Pope or by the Bishop of the diocese, or by their authority.

In the absence, however, of an approved priest, a person in danger of death may be validly absolved by any priest, bad or good, heretic, schismatic, apostate, or ex-communicated ; the Church in such a case supplies the needed jurisdiction.

260. The Effects of the Sacrament of Penance.—The effects of the Sacrament of Penance, rightly received, are these :—

(1) We are freed from the guilt of sin.

(2) Our souls are clothed with sanctifying grace.

In other words, we are justified; for the Sacrament of Penance is the channel by which God the Holy Ghost restores His justice, righteousness or grace, and charity to the soul that has lost it after Baptism by committing mortal sin.

(3) God remits the whole of the eternal punishment which our sins deserved.

(4) He remits more or less of the temporal punishment due to our sins, in proportion to the fervour with which we repent and perform our penance.

(5) He forgives us the venial sins of which we repent.

(6) He gives us a sort of right or claim upon Himself for actual graces, in time of need, to avoid sin and to conquer temptations.

(7) He restores to us the merits of the good works which we had previously done in grace and had lost by falling into mortal sin.

(8) And He commonly gives us great peace of mind and spiritual consolation.

261. When to receive the Sacrament.— We are bound to receive this Sacrament, *after falling into mortal sin—*
(1) When in danger of death ;
(2) Before receiving Confirmation or Matrimony, or any other Sacrament ; unless we can certainly make an act of perfect contrition ;
(3) Always before receiving Holy Communion ;
(4) And, therefore, every Easter, in order to fulfil aright the Easter precept.

We do well to receive it every week, or at least every three or four weeks, even if no mortal sin has stained our soul ; and after mortal sin as soon as we possibly can.

For to remain in the guilt of mortal sin is to despise God's loving invitations to repent and be pardoned ; to despise His threats ; to run the risk of sinning more grievously, and of forming almost unconquerable habits of sin ; to endanger our eternal salvation ; and to rob God of glory that we ought to give Him.

Not that God gains no glory by a soul that is lost ; for His justice must needs be glorified by the eternal punishment of evil. But the glory that delights Him is the glory that is freely given Him by the worship of a sanctified soul ; and of this He is robbed by those who remain in sin.

EXTREME UNCTION.

262. Our Lord, on one occasion, sent forth His Apostles, two by two, to preach ; and after He had given them instructions, "Going forth they preached that [people] should do penance ; and they cast out many devils, and *anointed with oil* many that were sick, and healed them " (Mark vi. 12, 13).

It was either then, or later on, that He instituted the Sacrament of "the last anointing," or Extreme Unction.

For St. James, in his Epistle (v. 14, 15), says : " Is any man sick among you ? let him bring in the priests of the Church ; and let them pray over him, anointing him with oil in the name of the Lord : and the prayer of faith shall save the sick man, and the Lord shall raise him up, and if he be in sins, they shall be forgiven him."

263. By whom and how Extreme Unction is given.—From St. James's words, it is clear that a priest alone is the minister of this Sacrament.

And the word "priest" means not a mere elder or senior, but one having power from Christ through the Sacrament of Holy Order.

In giving Extreme Unction the priest anoints the eyes, ears, nostrils, lips, hands, and sometimes the feet of the sick person, at the same time saying : " By this holy unction, and His own most tender mercy, may the Lord forgive thee whatever by sight (*or* by hearing, smell, taste and speech, touch, *or* step) thou hast done amiss."

This form, however, is preceded, if time permit, and followed, by many beautiful prayers befitting the occasion.

The oil used in the anointing is pure oil of olives that has been blessed by the Bishop on Maundy Thursday.

264. Who may or may not receive Extreme Unction.—This Sacrament is only for those who have sinned, and are sick unto death, that is, in danger of death through their sickness.

Thus it may not be given to criminals before execution, nor to soldiers before battle, nor to sailors or travellers before a dangerous voyage ; nor to infants or idiots who have never, from their want of reason, been capable of sinning.

But to all other Catholics in danger of death by old age, or by sickness, this Sacrament may be given.

It may even be given to those that are delirious, that have been stunned and rendered senseless by accident, or by drowning, poisoning, or violence, in cases of attempted suicide, whenever it is not certain that the sinner is dying impenitent; for in most of such cases there is just the possibility that the dying sinner may be sensible, though speechless, and that the departing soul may have made, or may make, by the grace of God, through the prayer of the Church, at the moment when the Sacrament is given, an act, unknown to the by-standers, of true repentance.

Of course to one evidently dying in final impenitence no Sacrament may be given.

265. At what time to receive it.—When a Catholic is taken seriously ill, the priest should at once be sent for.

There is no harm in sending too soon; whereas it is dangerous to wait, and certainly sinful, both for him that is sick, and for them that attend him, not to send for the priest until death is at hand.

This Sacrament should be received *as soon as there is a probable danger of death*. And that for two reasons : (1) that he who is sick may make due preparation to receive it worthily, whilst he has all his senses ; and (2) because this Sacrament often acts like a natural remedy, and when received in time restores strength to the body, should the good of the soul require it. "The Lord shall raise him up." But we have no right to delay until human remedies have failed, and then expect the Sacrament to work a miracle.

266. How to prepare for it.—The best preparation for Extreme Unction is, (1) if possible, to make a good confession, and (2) if convenient, to receive the Holy Viaticum.

If confession cannot be made, and the soul be in mortal sin, the essential preparation is an act of true repentance, at least an act of attrition.

In any case there should also be acts of Faith, Hope, Charity, and Resignation to the holy will of God.

267. The Effects of Extreme Unction.—

Should any one receive this Sacrament who is in mortal sin, but either unconscious of his sinful state, or unable to confess by word or sign, and yet truly sorry for all his mortal sins, such a one is forgiven, and justified by the instrumentality of this Sacrament.

Should any one in mortal sin receive this Sacrament in a state of total unconsciousness, he would doubtless be justified by it, supposing he had previously made an act of true repentance, which remained unrevoked by later mortal sin.

There are strong theological reasons for these two statements, although doubtless this Sacrament was not intended by Christ, as a rule, to convey pardon for mortal sin.

This Sacrament was instituted, *in the first place*, to strengthen the soul in its agony against the attacks and temptations of the devil, which are then more violent than ever; *in the second place*, to dispose the soul for entrance into glory, by the remission of venial sins and the temporal punishments due for all; *in the third place*, to banish unreasonable fears, anxiety, despairing thoughts, or spiritual sloth, as the case may be, which are the remains of sin; and, *in the fourth place*, supposing God sees it good for the soul, to restore, for a time at least, consciousness and more or less perfect recovery.

So, in short, the effects of this Sacrament are:—Grace, remission of sins, liberation from temporal punishment, spiritual peace, comfort, and assistance against temptations, and, if need be, the alleviation of bodily sickness.

268. How to Help the Dying.—When any one is in danger of death the first duty is to tell him so. It is a cruelty and a crime not to let him know his danger, whatever the doctor may sometimes say to the contrary.

If the danger is not immediate, get him first to settle his affairs; to make his will, if need be; to arrange his family matters; to pay his debts, and to be reconciled to his enemies, if he have any.

Send for a priest as soon as possible.

Read or say prayers with the sick person; especially Acts of Contrition.

(School-children ought to be taught to do these things. When taught, they can often do them better than grown-up people. Sometimes friends and neighbours can do them better than near relations).

When the priest is coming to give Holy Viaticum, prepare for him as directed in *art.* 242.

If he is coming to give Extreme Unction also, he will want some water in a basin, a clean towel, and a piece of bread crumb upon a plate. These things should be in readiness for him in the sick person's room.

When the sick person is actually dying, and the priest is not present, some one should read the Prayers for a Departing Soul.

269. How to help a Dying Protestant.—When a Protestant is dying, any Catholic, man, woman, or child, may help him to save his soul.

Tell him about the passion and death of Christ;

How *his* sins helped to murder Christ;

How God is worthy to be loved and served for His goodness and mercy.

In other words, suggest to him all the motives of Perfect Contrition.

Make for him acts of Faith in Christ, and in the truths of Faith, as far as he knows them; acts of Hope for the proper motives; and acts of Perfect Contrition.

270. Other Recommendations about the Sick.—(1) Be always patient, kind, and generous with the sick.

Let nurses tend them with careful modesty.

Let none but good people come near the dying.

Let there be in their hearing no foolish or worldly talk.

Let a Crucifix or pious picture hang before them.

(2) Take care not to catch their disease.

Take care not to breathe their breath.

Keep the sick room always neat and perfectly clean.

Keep it warm, with a fire if need be, but open the window sometimes to let in fresh air.

As to food and medicine, do exactly as the doctor orders.

HOLY ORDER.

271. From various parts of the New Testament we may gather that Our Lord conferred upon the Apostles, at some time or other, the following spiritual powers and privileges :—

(1) Of offering the Eucharistic Sacrifice (1 Cor. xi. 24, 25).

(2) Of distributing Communion to the faithful (Luke xxii. 19).

(3) Of forgiving and retaining sins (John xx. 23).

(4) Of binding and loosing, not only sins, but other things "whatsoever" (Mat. xviii. 18).

(5) Of baptising (Mat. xxviii. 19).

(6) Of imparting the Holy Ghost (Acts viii. 17).

(7) Of anointing the sick for their pardon and recovery (James v. 14, 15).

(8) Of preaching His Gospel to every creature (Mark xvi. 15, Rom. x. 15), and of teaching all nations His commands (Mat. xxviii. 20).

(9) Of ruling the Church (Acts xx. 28).

(10) Of communicating these powers separately to other men, by what is called Ordination, or the Sacrament of Holy Order; or, in other words, of ordaining Deacons and Priests, and consecrating Bishops (Acts i. 26 ; vi. 5, 6 : Titus i. 5).

272. The Sacred Orders.—A Bishop is one who has received all the above-named powers.

A Priest is one who has received power to offer the Eucharistic Sacrifice, and to forgive sins; and, with these, the power also to give Extreme Unction, to preach and teach the word of God, and to minister to the flock of Christ in many other ways.

A Deacon is one who has received the power to assist the priest in celebrating Mass, and in certain cases to preach and administer solemn Baptism.

In the days of the Apostles almost every priest was a Bishop too; and hence in Scripture, and in some very early writings, the word *Priest* often means *High-Priest* or *Bishop*.

The Episcopate, or office of a Bishop, is indeed only the plenitude or fulness of the priesthood.

273. How these Orders are Conferred.—The Bishop confers the Sacrament of Order, or passes on from Christ the above-named powers, by placing his hands on the recipient's head (Acts vi. 6; xiii. 3; 2 Tim. i. 6), by delivering, with suitable words, the instruments of the sacred office conferred, and by prayer.

274. The Effects of Holy Order.—That the laying on of hands in the act of ordaining confers the special grace of the Holy Ghost, together with special spiritual power, is evident from Acts xiii. 3; 1 Tim. iv. 14; 2 Tim. i. 6.

That it also stamps an indelible mark or character upon the soul, like the character of Baptism and Confirmation, and gives it a certain right or claim to divine assistance in the performance of sacred duties, is the doctrine and tradition of the Church.

275. The Preparatory Orders.—Besides the Episcopate, the Priesthood, and the Diaconate there are other preparatory orders, which are not of Divine, but of only ecclesiastical origin.

These are the orders of Sub-Deacon, Acolythe, Exorcist, Lector, and Ostiarius or Door-keeper.

And before these comes the Tonsure, a ceremony by which a man is made a cleric.

Each of these so-called Minor Orders is conferred by the Bishop with holy and grace-giving rites, which impart power and authority to exercise certain functions; but these rites are not Sacraments, for they lack the institution of Christ.

By law, however, in the Latin Church, the Sub-diaconate is counted among the Sacred Orders, and, therefore, one who receives it is bound to perpetual celibacy, and the recitation of the Divine Office.

276. The Celibacy of the Clergy.—All
Bishops, priests, deacons, and sub-deacons, who use the Latin rite, are bound, not by Divine command, but by the law of the Church, to lead lives of perpetual chastity.

No man can marry, therefore, after he has taken the sub-diaconate.

This law is most ancient, being certainly of Apostolical, though not of Divine origin.

The following are some of the reasons why the clergy are commanded never to marry, and never to live with their wives after taking the sub-diaconate, if they were previously married :—

(1) Chastity is a virtue most highly praised in Holy Scripture, and most pleasing to God.

Our Lord says,—" Amen, I say to you, there is no man that hath left house, or parents, or brethren, or *wife*, or children for the kingdom of God's sake, who shall not receive much more in this present time, and in the world to come life everlasting" (Luke xviii. 29).

St. John saw in Revelation, " a hundred and forty-four thousand " celibates, having Christ's name " and the name of His Father written on the foreheads," and harpers, singing, " as it were, a new song," and no man could learn the song save the hundred and forty-four thousand;" "and these are they who were not defiled with women; for they are virgins" (Apoc. xiv. 1—5).

St. Paul says, "A Bishop must be. . . . sober, just, holy, and continent," that is, pure (1 Titus i. 8); tells Timothy to be an example, amongst other things, "in chastity" (1 Tim. iv. 12); and says many things in praise of virginity in 1 Cor. vii.

The Church, therefore, thinks that no man is fitted for the "ministry of reconciliation" unless he is detached from earthly things and natural pleasures and family cares.

(2) The example of our Blessed Lord, the example of His Holy Mother, the example of the Virgin Disciple, the example of St. Paul, the example, in fact, of all the Apostles, who were either never married at all, or, at least as far as we know, never lived as the married live, from the time when their ministry began —all this is an argument for the law of celibacy.

And (3) Experience. The Church has married as well as unmarried priests.

The Catholic Greek clergy who marry before they become deacons are allowed by the Church to retain their wives; and the contrast between them and the unmarried clergy, in point of spiritual usefulness, is a powerful argument for the universal law of celibacy.

277. Vocation.—"You have not chosen Me, but I have chosen you" (John xv. 16), said our Blessed Lord to the first priests of His Church.

So in Heb. v. 4, it is said, "Neither doth any man take the honour to himself, but he that is called by God, as Aaron was."

And, therefore, in order that one may be a good priest, it is needful that he enter "by the door" (John x. 1), which is Christ; in other words, that he be called by the voice of God.

And the usual signs of a call from God are such as these:—

An inclination to serve God in the priesthood;

A previous good life;

A desire, not of honour or gain, but to give God greater glory;

A zeal for the salvation of souls;

And a love of prayer, of spiritual reading, and of sacred studies.

278. Conditions for Ordination.—Besides the signs of a Divine vocation, the Church requires:—

That the candidate have been confirmed;

That he be in the state of grace;

That he have no canonical impediment;

That he be sufficiently instructed;

That he be of the proper canonical age;

That he undertake all the obligations and responsibilities of the order he is about to receive;

And that certain intervals of time elapse between the reception at least of the sacred orders.

But for some of these conditions, in case of urgency, the Bishop or the Pope has a dispensing power.

MATRIMONY, OR MARRIAGE.

279. Marriage is a contract by which an unmarried man and an unmarried woman engage, at a particular moment, to be, from that time forward, man and wife.

Our Lord Jesus Christ has made this contract a Sacrament.

This is clear (1) from our Lord's own words, "What God hath joined together" (Mat. xix. 6), marriage thus being the work of God, and not of the contracting parties only; (2) from the unvarying teaching of the Church in every age; and (3) from the fact that Christ has laid upon those who enter the married state, obligations so strict and so hard to fulfil, that a special Sacrament is needed to give married people the grace to fulfil them.

But whether Christ made it a Sacrament when He went to the marriage at Cana (John ii.) or when He decreed that it should be indissoluble (Mat. xix. 6), or after His Resurrection, when speaking of the kingdom of God (Acts i. 3), is not clear from Holy Scripture.

280. What constitutes a Marriage.— The one thing necessary to make a valid marriage is the agreement of the contracting parties, whether made by words or by signs, to take each other, there and then, and until death shall part them, for husband and wife.

From which two things are clear : (1) that the bridegroom is the minister of this Sacrament to the bride, and the bride to the bridegroom ; and (2) that marriage is *indissoluble ;* that is to say, that nothing but the death of one of the parties can free the other from the obligations which the marriage tie involves.

These obligations are as follow :—

(1) That they yield to each other in all that is lawful in the sight of God unto the birth of offspring ;

(2) That they love and be faithful to each other ;

(3) That they feed, clothe, and educate their children, and bring them up in the fear of God ;

(4) That they live together, and, as far as is needful, work for each other's assistance ;

(5) That the wife be in reason, and in things not sinful, obedient to her husband.

These obligations remain in force, binding each party, until one of them is known for certain to be dead. See Rom. vii. 2.

They are explained at length by St. Paul in 1 Cor. v., vi., vii. ; Eph. v. 22, 23 ; by St. Peter, in his First Epistle, iii., 1—7 ; and in many other parts of Holy Scripture.

See also the explanation of the Fourth Commandment.

281. The Indissolubility of the Marriage Tie.—Our Blessed Lord laid down the law once and for all : " What God hath joined together let no man put asunder " (Mat. xix. 6).

And, therefore, everyone that putteth away his wife, and marrieth another, committeth adultery; and he that marrieth her that is put away from her husband committeth adultery" (Luke xvi. 18).

Divorce, then, in its common meaning of a separation, with leave to each to marry another party, is always impossible. It can neither be effected by mutual consent, nor by court of law, nor by any power on earth.

The cruelty or adultery of one of the parties indeed is a reason for a temporary separation. But even in such unhappy cases, "Not I," says St. Paul, "but the Lord commandeth, that the wife depart not from her husband; and if she depart that she remain unmarried, or be reconciled to her husband" (1 Cor. vii. 10, 11).

Moreover, besides the will of Christ, which is law to the Christian, there are many good reasons for not dissolving the bond of marriage.

These are found in the neglect of children, the utter ruin of morals, the murders, and other fearful crimes, which have followed, and must needs follow, from the practice of divorce.

282. Impediments to Marriage.—Impediments to matrimony are certain circumstances, which, either from the nature of the case, or from the express revelation of God, or by the laws of the Church, prevent certain people either from being married at all, or at least from receiving this Sacrament lawfully and worthily.

Those hindrances to marriage, which render the contract null and void, are called *diriment impediments*.

Those hindrances which only render the marriage unlawful and sinful are called *impedient impediments*.

283. Diriment Impediments.—No man can marry any relative in a direct line, such as his mother or grandmother, daughter, or grand-daughter; nor any blood-relation within the fourth degree, as, for instance, his niece, or his first, second, or third cousin. Nor can any woman marry a man similarly related to her.

No widower can marry his deceased wife's sister, or any one related by blood to his deceased wife within the fourth degree. Nor can any widow marry a man similarly related to her deceased husband, as, for instance, her deceased husband's brother.

Relationship by blood is called *Consanguinity*: and the relationship of a man to all the blood-relations of his wife, or of a woman to all the blood-relations of her husband, is called *Affinity*.

No two persons can marry between whom there exists any spiritual relationship (see *arts*. 203, 220).

No man in sacred orders can marry; nor can any man or woman who has taken a *solemn* vow of chastity in a religious order, or a *simple* vow of chastity in the Society of Jesus.

No Catholic can marry an unbaptised person.

No man can have more than one wife; no woman more than one husband; polygamy and polyandria being both against nature, and absolutely forbidden by the law of Christ.

No one once married can marry again without *proof* of the other party's death.

In certain Catholic countries, where a decree of the Council of Trent to this effect has been published, no marriage is valid unless it takes place before the parish priest and two witnesses.

No foreigner from a Catholic country can be validly married in England without the leave of his own parish priest, unless such foreigner has come, not as a visitor merely, but to take up his abode and make his home here, at least for a considerable time; or unless, as they say in law, he has acquired here a *domicile* or *quasi-domicile*.

These diriment impediments are intended to prevent the Sacrament of Marriage from being the occasion of either physical evil, injustice, or crime.

Due regard being paid to the dignity of the Sacrament, and to the rights of all parties concerned, the Church can sometimes dispense from such impediments as consanguinity, in the second or third degrees, and of affinity in the first degree, should any grave reason require it.

But from some of the diriment impediments the Church has no power to dispense.

284. Impedient Impediments.—Impedient impediments are such as render marriage unlawful and sinful, at least for the time being.

Thus it is sinful, from the nature of the case, to break a promise of marriage, and much more sinful to break a solemn engagement to marry, without grave reason, and then to marry another party.

It is grievously sinful to marry before a civil registrar only, or before a Protestant minister, or in any other way than before a priest and two witnesses, as the Church directs.

It is sinful to solemnise marriage between Ash Wednesday and Low Sunday, inclusively, and between the first Sunday of Advent and the feast of the Epiphany, inclusively. No Nuptial Mass, or solemn blessing of the married pair, is allowed during these times, and no marriage ought really to take place within them.

It is sinful to marry in violation of any vow of chastity, or of entering a religious order.

And, lastly, it is strictly forbidden to contract a mixed marriage, that is, for a Catholic to marry a Protestant.

As to times, vows, and mixed marriages, however, the Bishops have power, in cases of need, to dispense from the ordinary law.

285. Banns.—The banns, or the announcement of every intended marriage, must be published in Church, at the principal Mass, on three consecutive

Sundays, or Holy Days, in the mission where the parties reside.

If the parties be of different missions, the banns must be published in each.

The banns are published in order that both the contracting parties, and the priest who blesses the marriage, may be practically certain, when the marriage takes place, that there is no impediment to it.

If the marriage be not contracted within two months after the publication of the banns, they must be published again, unless the Bishop dispense from them.

Any Christian, of whatever age or sex, who knows of an impediment to the marriage of any two persons, is bound to make it known when the banns of marriage between those persons are published.

A lawyer or doctor, however, who knows of such impediment as a professional secret, is bound only to admonish the parties themselves.

286. Mixed Marriages.—A mixed marriage is a marriage between a Catholic and a baptised person who is not a Catholic.

A mixed marriage is always an evil; although out of this, as out of other evils, God sometimes brings forth good.

Sometimes, however, a mixed marriage may be the less of two evils.

Sometimes a person must either marry a Protestant, or remain unmarried, and that perhaps in poverty, or in grave danger of sin.

In such cases of real necessity, the Church, if applied to, will grant a dispensation, that is, take away the prohibition, and make the marriage lawful.

But observe, in every case where an impediment is known to exist, it is unlawful and sinful to make an absolute promise of marriage until a dispensation *has been* obtained.

In the case of mixed marriages, the Bishop can grant a dispensation, and the Catholic party can lawfully marry, *only* on the following conditions :—

(1) That *all* the children that may be born of the marriage shall be baptised, and brought up in the Catholic Faith ;

(2) That the Catholic party shall have full liberty to practise the Catholic religion ;

(3) That no religious ceremony shall take place elsewhere than in the Catholic Church.

These conditions should, if possible, be written and signed by both parties. The first of them is exacted because a Catholic parent can neither give up the right, nor escape the *duty*, of bringing up all his or her children in the way of salvation, which is only to be found in the Catholic Church. The justice and necessity of the second condition are evident. And as to the third, the marriage of a Catholic before a Protestant minister is a participation in an act of false religion, " an implicit adhesion to heresy," as the Holy See has declared, and, therefore, a sacrilege.

Finally, the Catholic party is bound in charity to strive by prayer, by word, and by good example, to lead the other into the bosom of God's Church.

287. How to Marry Well.—To marry well —in the sight of God—is to receive the Sacrament of Marriage worthily.

This can only be done by long and careful preparation : a more careful preparation being needed to receive this Sacrament worthily than to receive any other, except perhaps Holy Orders.

The proper preparation for matrimony consists of all, or, at any rate, of most, of the following acts, which for brevity sake are expressed as admonitions.

I. Remote Preparations.—Catholic Youth or Maiden ! (1) Lead a good life ; for " A good wife is a good portion ; she shall be given in the portion of them that fear God, to a man *for his good deeds* " (Ecclus. xxvi. 3). And the like may be said of a good husband.

(2) When you have come to an age to think about marriage, pray that God may give you a good Catholic wife or husband, as the case may be.

(3) In making your choice be guided by Faith and by common sense. Look first and foremost to moral character. Consult your parents, your priest, your older and more prudent friends. It is lawful sometimes to marry against the likings and wishes of parents, but hardly ever against their reasonable objections.

(4) Let your courtship be pure and modest from beginning to end. For absolute modesty and perfect purity before the marriage-day will bring unfailing mutual love, joy, and happiness after.

(5) Marry for a good intention; that you may make and be made happy " in the Lord," and may raise up children to be citizens of the kingdom of God.

II. Immediate Preparation.—About a month before the appointed marriage-day, give notice to the priest about the banns, and to the registrar, in order to comply with the law of the land. The law requires a notice of twenty-one clear days to be given to the registrar.

Then, having arranged with the priest the day and hour of the marriage, request the registrar, whose presence is required by law, to be present in the church at the said day and hour.

In the meantime prepare your soul for the reception of so great a Sacrament, which is a figure of Christ's union with His Church (Eph. v. 30—32).

Obtain instruction, if need be, either in the general truths and duties of religion, or in the nature and obligations of this Sacrament.

On the night before the marriage, if possible, make a good confession.

On the morning of the marriage, during the Nuptial Mass, receive the Blessed Eucharist, and thus, with the blessing of God, in the state of grace, commence your married life.

288. The Marriage Service.—This commences with two questions put by the priest, as to the willingness of the bridegroom and bride to take each other for lawful wife and husband.

On each answering in the affirmative, the bridegroom takes the hand of the bride, and declares that he takes her for his wedded wife from that day forward until death.

Then the bride takes the hand of the bridegroom, and makes a similar declaration: that she takes him for her wedded husband until death.

In these two declarations lies the whole of the contract and Sacrament of Matrimony.

Then the bridegroom lays down a piece of money, and the ring, which the priest proceeds to bless.

After the blessing of the ring, the bridegroom says, "With this ring I thee wed: this gold and silver I thee give: with my body I thee worship; and with all my worldly goods I thee endow;" and places the ring on the bride's fingers, "In the name of the Father, and of the Son, and of the Holy Ghost. Amen."

The priest then prays aloud for the married couple, and he proceeds to celebrate—

289. The Nuptial Mass.—The Nuptial Mass is either the *Missa pro Sponso et Sponsa*, for the bridegroom and bride; or else the Mass of the Sunday, Holy Day of Obligation, or "double of the first or second class," as the greater feasts are called, on which the marriage may be solemnised; with special prayers, however, for the married couple from the Mass *Pro Sponso et Sponsa*.

At the *Pater Noster* the priest turns towards the married couple, and says two prayers over them, one especially for the bride, which prayers the married pair and the bystanders will do well to follow in an English translation.

And, lastly, the priest invokes another special blessing on them, just before the usual blessing of the people.

There is no obligation to have a Nuptial Mass; yet no two Catholics who are making a holy union, with nothing to be ashamed of, and hoping for the blessing of God upon their mutual love, will, through indecent haste, or a foolish fear of a little natural nervousness, have the Nuptial Mass omitted.

290. The Graces of this Sacrament.—These are, (1) an increase of sanctifying grace at the moment of the marriage, and (2) in after times actual graces to enable them to love and be faithful to each other, to stand by each other in time of need, to resist temptations, and to bring up their children in the knowledge, love, and fear of God.

The Doctrine of the Church on the Sacraments in General.

291. This doctrine is contained chiefly in the Instruction for the Armenians issued by the Council of Florence, under Pope Eugenius IV., A.D. 1439, and in the Canons and Decrees of the Council of Trent.

1. In the practical Instruction to the Armenians the Council of Florence taught as follows:—

That the Sacraments of the New Law are seven in number:

That they contain grace (not physically, of course, as a cup contains water, but instrumentally, as a sword may be said to have death in it), and impart grace to such as receive them worthily:

That Baptism, Confirmation, Holy Eucharist, Penance, and Extreme Unction have been instituted for the spiritual perfection of every man; Order and Matrimony for the spiritual government and the multplication of the Church at large:

That by Baptism we are spiritually born again; that by Confirmation we are increased in grace and strengthened in faith; that, after being so re-born and strengthened, we are nourished and fed by the Holy Eucharist; that, if our souls have become diseased by sin, we are spiritually healed by Penance; that we are spiritually healed, and even bodily, should the good of the soul require it, by Extreme Unction; and that by Order the Church is governed and multiplied spiritually, and by Matrimony multiplied bodily.

2. The Instruction proceeds to say:—

That all the Sacraments are made up (1) of things which are, as it were, their *matter*, (2) of words which are, as it were, their *form*, and (3) of the person of the minister who confers the Sacrament with the intention of doing what the Church does;

And that, if anything of these three things be wanting there is no Sacrament. To this, however, in respect of *matter*, the Instruction implies two exceptions.

For it teaches, in detail, later on, that the matter of Baptism is natural water, cold or warm; that the matter of Confirmation is chrism; that the matter of the Eucharist is wheaten bread and wine from the grape, mixed with a little water; that the matter of Extreme Unction is olive oil, blessed by a bishop; that the matter of Order is that, by the handing of which the order is conferred.

But under the Sacrament of Penance it speaks of the penitent's acts—Contrition, Confession, and Satisfaction—as the *quasi materia*, or the " so-to-say matter," of the Sacrament;

And in the case of Matrimony, it mentions neither matter nor form, but simply says that the " efficient cause of matrimony, as a rule, is mutual consent, expressed by words there and then."

In fact, neither in Penance nor in Matrimony is there anything used as a part of the external sign which corresponds, say, to the water used in Baptism.

In every Sacrament, however, there are words used which express the meaning of the ceremony and indicate its spiritual effect; and these words are the *form* of the Sacrament; perhaps in Penance and Matrimony the *matter* also.

3. The Instruction to the Armenians teaches that Baptism, Confirmation, and Order imprint upon the soul a *character*, or a certain spiritual sign, or mark, or seal, which is distinct for each Sacrament, and can never be blotted out of the soul.

4. The Council of Trent has confirmed all the doctrine contained in the above-named Instruction, and has also taught :—

That some of these Sacraments are necessary, at least in desire, for salvation; these, of course, are Baptism for all, Penance for such as have mortally sinned after Baptism, and the others for some men only in certain cases:

That the Sacraments contain the grace which they signify, and confer it upon all who do not place an obstacle in the way of it; as, for instance, by going to confession without proper repentance, by going to Communion in mortal sin, or by trying to get married with an impediment:

That the Sacraments give grace of themselves, *ex opere operato*, that is, on account of the action performed, which action is the action of Christ repeated by His ministers.

5. To understand this it must be borne in mind :—

That the Sacraments are actions, consisting of something said, and something done, by the command of Christ, as Christ Himself once did it, or showed the way to do it:

That these sacramental actions are now done by men, who, in doing them, are merely deputies and ministers of Christ:

That the hand and mouth of the minister indeed are the hand and mouth of man, but the real voice that speaks, and the power that works, are God's:

That the grace which the Sacraments give is the fruit, not of man's prayer or good acts, but of Christ's Precious Blood:

And that this grace is conferred in the Sacraments by the Holy Ghost, who is present and works in and through them.

6. And hence we may see why the Council of Trent could teach :—

That there must indeed be an appointed minister, since all Christians have not the power from Christ to act in His name :

And that the minister must intend, when giving a Sacrament, *at least* to do what the Church does :

But that the Sacraments are good and valid, and convey their grace to the recipient, however sinful the minister may be, provided he perform the essential action of the Sacrament, that is, use the due matter and form.

7. The Church also teaches, at least by the common consent of her pastors :—

That all the Sacraments were instituted by Christ, though Scripture has not in all cases recorded His act of institution :

That no Apostle, Pope, Bishop, priest, or layman of any kind has ever had power to institute a Sacrament, that is, to make earthly signs the infallible channel of heavenly grace :

That all the Sacraments confer sanctifying or habitual grace, by which the soul is made holy or holier :

That each of them confers this grace for some particular purpose, to make us holy or holier in some particular way, to fit us for some particular state of life, or to give us some special power ; that each of them, therefore, is a sort of covenant, or compact, in which God engages to give us, in time of need, certain corresponding actual graces ; and that all grace thus given, or directed to a particular purpose by any Sacrament, is called *Sacramental Grace :*

That two Sacraments only, Baptism and Penance, are intended to make us holy, that is, to wash away mortal sin, and to give us grace when we have none ; and these two Sacraments, because we can receive them when our souls are dead to grace, and buried in mortal sin, are called the *Sacraments of the dead ;*

That all the other Sacraments are called *the Sacraments of the living*, because they are intended only to increase our holiness, and must be received when our souls are already holy, or living to God, in the state of grace :

And that every Sacrament, being a morally certain means of grace, is a pledge of God's love, and care, and forethought for us ; and to receive them worthily is the greatest happiness in the world.

292. The Use of Sacred Ceremonies.—

Our Lord once said—" This do for a commemoration of Me." And the principle involved in these words goes through the whole system of the Catholic religion.

The Sacraments are sacred rites or actions which take the mind straight back to Christ—to Christ working, Christ healing, Christ forgiving sins, Christ dying on the cross.

They commemorate Christ and all His teachings.

For in the simple sacramental acts themselves, and in the more elaborate ceremonial with which, when possible, from the very times of the Apostles, these acts have been accompanied, all Gospel Truth is involved, implied, and suggested (see Art. 90).

So also with the great Sacrifice of the Mass.

Christ, who so loved us, worked for us, taught us Truth, showed us how to live and how to die, and offered Himself an atoning sacrifice for our sins, becomes bodily there—a commemoration of Himself.

And, therefore, does the priest at the altar, and, therefore, do they who attend him, use many a sacred rite, that is, many an outward expression of inward faith, hope, adoration, and love.

Thus the Church's public worship of God, through sacred rites and ceremonies, is verily " worship in spirit and in truth'" (John iv. 23) ; for (1) it is a worship in which the whole man acts—his body with its senses, and his soul with its memory, reason, and will ; (2) it is a worship which excites devotion by its beauty and majesty; and (3) it is a worship by which Truth is taught and Christ is preached.

293. Sacramentals.—These are certain means by which we can participate in the merits of the Church's prayers and good works.

We can do this, for instance, (1) by using the prayers of the Church, as the Lord's Prayer, the Confiteor, the prayers at Mass, and the Divine Office; (2) by reading the Holy Scriptures; (3) by receiving personally the blessing of the Church; (4) by using piously things which the Church has blessed; and (5) by the frequent use of the Sign of the Cross.

294. Personal Blessings.—These are:—
The Blessings used in conferring the Minor Orders;
The Exorcisms used in Baptism;
The Blessings in the Marriage Service;
In fact, all the ceremonies (except the *matter* and *form*) used in conferring any Sacrament;
The salutations (Dominus Vobiscum), the ceremonies, and the Blessing in Holy Mass;
The Blessing of women before and after child-birth; and various others.

295. Blessed Things.—The Church blesses "by the word of God and prayer" (1 Tim. iv. 5), "every creature," or created thing, that is to be used in the administration of the Sacraments.

Thus three holy oils are blessed and used by the Church; the oil of Catechumens, by which children are anointed immediately before their Baptism, and priests at their Ordination; the chrism (olive oil mixed with balsam), used in Confirmation, and in the consecration of a Bishop; and the oil for anointing the sick in Extreme Unction.

The Church also blesses *water*, and by blessing it makes it *holy water*, and prays in the blessing of it that it may put to flight demons, drive away diseases, and free the houses and property of the faithful, wherever it is sprinkled, from all uncleanness and harm, pestilent spirits, noxious air, and other dangerous influences.

The Church also blesses candles on Candlemas-day, for a similar use; ashes on Ash-Wednesday, which are placed upon our foreheads to remind us that we are dust, and that unto dust we must return; and palms on Palm-Sunday, which are given us in remembrance of our Lord's triumphal entry into Jerusalem.

The Church also has blessings for churches, that all who pray therein may find mercy; for houses, that the angel of God may dwell therein, and protect them; for bread, eggs, fruit, and anything else to eat or drink, that they may contribute to the health both of body and soul, of all that receive them; and for many other things.

296. The Sign of the Cross.—The Sign of the Cross is a short profession of Faith.

By making it we "bless ourselves" "in the name of the Father, and of the Son, and of the Holy Ghost. Amen."

We thus profess our Faith in the Unity and Trinity of God, and in the virtue of our Blessed Lord's death upon the Cross; and we also express hope and trust that God will guard us, free us from danger and all evil, and forgive us our sins.

297. The Use and Effect of the Sacramentals.—Some of the Sacramentals, as the Lord's Prayer, and some other prayers, and perhaps the blessing of the Holy Oils, are of Divine origin.

Others, as the use of holy water, and the sign of the Cross, come down certainly from Apostolic times.

The rest are of later institution.

They are not Sacraments, because they lack either the institution of Christ, or His infallible promise of grace.

But yet, since our act, when we use any one of them, is not all our own, but, in great measure, the act and prayer of the Church, which Christ has made "glorious," not having spot or wrinkle, "but holy and without blemish" (Eph. v. 27), and, therefore, most pleasing to Him; it follows that such an act has an extra merit, above what it has as a good work, in itself, to cleanse us from venial sin, to free us from temporal punishment, and to impetrate grace.

CHAPTER VII.

THE PRECEPTS OF THE CHURCH.

298. These are rules and regulations laid down by the Sovereign Pontiff and the Bishops of the Church, for "the edification of the body of Christ."

We are bound in conscience to obey the Bishops of the Church, for our Lord said to them, "He that heareth you heareth Me, and he that despiseth you despiseth Me" (Luke x. 16).

On the Bishops themselves, and on priests, the Church imposes some hundreds of precepts; but on the laity it only imposes very few.

And these are all merely to determine in particular the time, or place, or manner, in which some duty is to be performed that has been in general commanded by God Himself.

299. The First Precept of the Church.— *To hear Mass on Sundays, and other great feasts called Holy Days of Obligation, and to do no servile work upon them.*

The Holy Days of Obligation commanded by the Church to be observed in England are Christmas-day, the Circumcision of our Lord or New Year's-day, the Epiphany or Twelfth-day, Ascension-day, Corpus Christi-day, SS. Peter and Paul's, the feast of our Lady's Assumption, and All Hallows' or All Saints'-day.

These days must therefore be kept holy, like Sundays. And what has been said in explanation of the Third Commandment of the Decalogue applies also to Holy Days of Obligation.

300. The Second Precept of the Church.
—*To fast on fasting-days, and to abstain from flesh meat on abstinence-days.*

The fasting days are—the forty days of Lent; the vigils, or eves, of Christmas-day, Pentecost, SS. Peter and Paul, the Assumption and All Saints; the Ember-days; and, in England, the Wednesdays and Fridays in Advent.

On the fasting-days all those who are over twenty-one years of age and under sixty, may only eat one full meal, and that after mid-day.

The Church, however, tacitly allows those who fast to take a little morning meal of bread, not more than two ounces, and an evening meal, not more than about eight ounces, of bread, fruit, fish, with such condiments as butter, cheese, and the like, as are not now forbidden by the law of abstinence.

The sick, and those who work hard, are not bound to fast.

The abstinence-days are days on which all people, young and old, except infants, are bound to abstain from eating flesh-meat.

The abstinence-days observed in England are—*all Fridays*, except the Friday on which Christmas-day may fall; and *all the fasting-days*, (except some in Lent, on which those who fast may eat flesh meat at dinner only, and those who are not of age to fast may eat it at any meal).

The sick, the poor, who have to eat what they can get, and those who would find it, for any other reason, a serious inconvenience to abstain, are not bound by this precept.

But in all cases of sickness, or inconvenience, it is well not to judge for ourselves, but to get a dispensation from our pastor, which will enable us to eat meat or to take full meals on the forbidden days without sin or scruple.

Drinking, as such, does not break the fast. To drink milk, however, thick chocolate, thick broth, or the like, is rather eating than drinking, and, therefore, breaks the fast when taken apart from the meals allowed.

As the laws of abstinence vary from time to time, and in different parts of the Church, they must be learned in detail from the particular instructions of the Bishop of the diocese, which are usually published in the churches on the Sunday before Ash-Wednesday.

301. The Object and Institution of Fasting.

—Fasting and abstinence are (1) acts of obedience, and (2) acts of mortification, by which we (1) honour God by obeying our divinely appointed superiors, at some inconvenience to ourselves, and (2) punish ourselves and satisfy God for our sins.

The first command given to men, and the only one given in the Garden of Eden, was one of abstinence : " Of the tree of knowledge, of good and evil, thou shalt not eat " (Gen. ii. 17).

In the Old Law fasting and different kinds of abstinence were frequently ordered and practised. For instance, the Nazarites had to abstain from wine (Num. vi. 2, 3); and all the Jews had, under pain of death, to abstain from eating the blood of any creature (Lev. vii. 26).

Our Saviour Himself fasted forty days (Mat. iv. 2).

He gave a rule and a reason for fasting in secret (see Mat. vi. 18).

The Apostles "ministered to the Lord and fasted" (Acts xiii. 2).

And they sent forth from Jerusalem the first precept issued by Church authority—"That you abstain from things sacrificed to idols, and from blood and from things strangled," &c. (Acts xv. 29).

But observe, all this fasting and abstinence rested not on the false principle that flesh or wine is evil in itself, a principle repudiated by St. Paul (1 Tim. iv. 1—3), but revived by some teetotalers, at least as regards wine and strong drinks, in these latter days; but it rested on the principle that "every one that striveth for the mastery, refraineth himself from all things" (1 Cor. ix. 25); for which reason St. Paul says, "I chastise my body and bring it into subjection" (ix. 27).

302. The other Precepts of the Church.
—These are merely regulations for the due reception of the Sacraments, and have been all explained in the chapter on the Sacraments.

They are as follow :—

To receive the Blessed Sacrament at least once a year, and that (in England) on some day in Lent, or within the octave of Easter, that is to say, between Ash-Wednesday and Low-Sunday.

To receive it (except as Viaticum) fasting from midnight.

And before receiving it, to be absolved in the Sacrament of Penance, from all mortal sins.

To go to confession at least once a year.

Not to marry within certain degrees of kindred; nor to marry non-Catholics; nor to marry, or attempt to marry, with any other impediment.

And, lastly, it is sometimes reckoned a precept of the Church, *To contribute to the support of the clergy, and the maintenance of religion.* But this is rather a Divine command. For St. Paul says, "*The Lord* hath ordained that they who preach the Gospel should live by the Gospel" (1 Cor. ix. 14). And, therefore, "Let him that is instructed in the word communicate to him that instructeth him in all good things" (Gal. vi. 6).

But, anyhow, all Catholics who can are certainly bound in conscience, (1) to pay Peter's Pence, according to the needs of the Sovereign Pontiff, and (2) to contribute to the support of their own immediate pastors.

CHAPTER VIII.

THE CHRISTIAN LIFE.

303. Our Obligations.—In our Baptism we "put on the new man, who, according to God, is created in *justice* and *holiness of truth*" (Eph. iv. 24).

In other words, we had a "new creature" (Gal. vi. 15) put into us, sanctifying grace and charity, poured into our souls "by the Holy Ghost" (Rom. v. 5), whereby we were "sealed into the day of redemption" (Eph. iv. 30).

But before this was done we had humbly to ask for Faith—that Faith that gives life everlasting.

We were told in reply to "keep the commandments" —to love God with our whole heart and soul and mind, and our neighbours as ourselves.

Then, after prayer, we had solemnly to renounce the devil and all his works, and pomps—sin, and that which leads to sin.

We had to declare our belief in God the Father, God the Son, and God the Holy Ghost, in the Holy Catholic Church, the Communion of Saints, the Forgiveness of Sins, the Resurrection of the Body, and Life Everlasting.

And then we were baptised—" washed," " sanctified," and " justified " (1 Cor. vi. 11)—that we might " walk in newness of life " (Rom. vi. 4).

304. The Working Out of Salvation.— We are, therefore, bound, under pain of damnation, to keep those promises made by us, or for us, at our Baptism.

For God commands us to keep them, even though they were only made in our name by our godfather and godmother, and made without our knowledge or consent.

We are, therefore, bound to keep ourselves " unspotted from this world " (Jas. i. 27), that is, to keep out of mortal sin, and to " watch and pray lest we enter into temptation " (Mat. xxvi. 41).

305. The Conquering of Sin. — Charity begins by conquering sin.

There are seven deadly vices, or habits of certain sins, which are deadly because they lead to other sins, and especially to the sins of apostasy and infidelity.

Against these the Christian must wage incessant war.

And the way to conquer them—to conquer our evil inclinations towards them—is to practise the opposite virtues.

Against PRIDE we must do acts of humility. We must bear in mind that we are creatures merely, owing all to God, having no rights before Him; in this world still, and not in hell, through His mercy alone; that thousands of people are better than we are, and thousands more would have been, if they had had our knowledge and grace; that whatever good we have is of God, and not of ourselves; that He has given to others more than to us—more talents, more learning, more knowledge, more beauty, more wealth, more ability to think and lead and rule; that, therefore, we may often be wrong, and need correcting, even by those below us;

that many gifts of God we have sinfully misused; and that, therefore, what we deserve for our ingratitude to God is, *at least*, contempt, neglect, and reproaches. We must, therefore, *act* upon all this truth, treat others as in *some sense* our betters; and when we suffer wrong, be patient, returning good for evil.

Against COVETOUSNESS, or Avarice, we must practise detachment; try not to grieve at losses or misfortunes; not set our heart on wealth, or honour, worshipping those instead of God; but give alms to the poor, and support religion.

Against LUST we must carefully avoid all persons, objects, amusements, unnecessary occupations, which excite temptation. In this matter cowardice is the only bravery, and flight the only fight. To this end, " I made a compact with my eyes," said the Wise Man in Scripture; and we must make a compact with our senses, never to look at, never to touch, never to *think* of, anything that excites impure inclinations. Purity has a guardian virtue, Modesty. And the only way to be pure is to be strictly modest—modest in thought, in word, in deed, in dress, and in all our ways before God and man.

Against ANGER we must strive to be truly humble, and practise every day to forgive slights and injuries, and to keep our temper when things go wrong. For the Christian rule is—" Love your enemies: do good to them that hate you," &c. (Mat. v. 44).

Against GLUTTONY and Drunkenness we must practise self-denial, eat and drink no more than is good for us. For one that has been given to drunkenness there is sometimes no remedy for his sin but an heroic pledge of total abstinence, at least for a time. Teetotalism, therefore, as a continuous act of self-denial, as a protest against prevalent drunkenness, as a reparation to God for the injuries done Him through drink, and as a good example to others whose only remedy is total abstinence, must needs in these days be a thing most pleasing to God.

Against ENVY we must love the brethren, wish well to all men, thank God for what He gives to other men, even to His enemies, or ours; and the less they thank Him for all His gifts, the more should we.

Against SLOTH we must perform our duties, especially our religious duties, with diligence and punctuality.

Thus, then, we must cure and avoid bad habits by forming good ones. There is found in the Gospel no homœopathic cure for sin.

306. The Way of Perfection.—But, further, not only bishops, priests, monks, and nuns, but all of us are in some way called "to be perfect as our heavenly Father is perfect" (Mat. v. 48).

We must strive to learn the spirit of Christ, and to follow His example, even in the smallest matters.

We must practise Christianity—practise it daily and hourly, as one practises a musical instrument. In other words, we must exercise all those virtues, or powers and dispositions to do good, which have been given us with sanctifying grace, and strengthen them by exercise.

Practice makes perfect.

307. The Theological Virtues.—We must live by FAITH. We must firmly believe all the truths of our holy religion. We must know our Faith well, and understand it. We must make frequent acts of Faith. We must preach it, too, at least "by kindly words and and virtuous life." We must glory in the Cross, the Gospel, and the Church of God.

We must always be guided in business, in politics, in every walk in life, by what Faith teaches to be right or wrong. And, lastly, our Faith must "work by Charity." Our Faith must tell us what to do, and our Love of God must make us do it.

It is only this kind of Faith that is worth a heavenly reward. For "Faith without works is dead" (Jas. ii. 20); and "by works a man is justified, and not

We must also live in HOPE, and trust, and confidence, that if we pray and keep God's Word, He will certainly reward us in the life to come.

We must, therefore, "pray without ceasing" (1 Thes. v. 17), by saying our formal prayers at stated times, by making very frequently short momentary acts of prayer and praise, by intending to do all we do for the honour of God, and by frequently offering our actions to Him, and so making all our life, even our sleep and recreations, one continued act of prayer and worship. "Do all in the name of the Lord Jesus Christ" (Col. iii. 17).

Above all, we must live in CHARITY. For of Faith, Hope, and Charity, "the greatest of these is Charity" (1 Cor. xiii. 13). For "God is CHARITY; and he that abideth in Charity abideth in God, and God in him" (1 John iv. 16).

We must prove, and at the same time exercise, our Charity by keeping the Commandments. "If you love me keep my Commandments" (John xiv. 15). "Let us love not in word, nor in tongue, but in deed, and in truth" (1 John iii. 1).

To be downright good Christians, real followers of Christ, we must, therefore, avoid, not only every mortal sin, but also every wilful venial sin. Moreover, at least in many things, we must go beyond what is commanded under pain of sin, and do, for the love of God, acts of virtue and piety which fall, there and then, under no particular precept, but only under those two general and all-embracing commandments, "Thou shalt love the Lord thy God with thy *whole* heart, with thy *whole* soul, with thy *whole* mind, and with thy *whole* strength," and "Thou shalt love thy neighbour as thyself" (Mark xii. 30, 31).

308. The Cardinal Virtues.—These are four, namely—Prudence, Justice, Fortitude, and Temperance.

They are called cardinal virtues (from the Latin word *cardo*, a hinge), because all other moral virtues

We are *prudent*, when we act with habitual prudence; when, in order to do all things well, we seek knowledge and information, take advice, are willing to be taught and guided by the experience of others; act with caution and forethought, and the pure intention of increasing the glory of God; and when we judge of men and things by the light of the Gospel, and measure them by the standard of Christ, and act towards all by the Gospel rules of conduct, namely, the Commandments of God and of the Church.

We are *just*, that is, morally upright and straightforward, when we give to every one his due; when we "render to Cæsar the things that are Cæsar's, and to God the things that are God's" (Mark xii. 17); when we pay to God His due service, honour, and worship; to His angels and saints due reverence; to our parents and superiors the love, honour, obedience, and support which is due to them respectively; when, if we are persons in authority, we duly reward the good and punish the wicked; when we pay our debts; when, if paid servants, we honestly do our work, and, if employers of labour, we pay fair wages to our servants and treat them kindly; when we feel and show gratitude for favours received; when we tell the truth always, never lying or deceiving our neighbour; when we faithfully carry out our lawful contracts; when in buying or selling we are guilty of no cheating, deception, or extortion; when we give to those in want; when we are affable, kind, and civil to all, according to states and circumstances.

We have *fortitude*, that is, we are brave and courageous, in a Christian sense, when we "contend earnestly for the Faith once delivered to the saints" (Jude i. 3); when we suffer patiently all evils, calumnies, reproaches for the name of Christ; when we bear with all the difficulties of our state in patient submission to the holy will of God.

We are *temperate*, when we resist the pleasures of our senses, so far as they allure us to evil; when especially we observe perfect purity according to our state; when we limit our eating and drinking to that which is needful to preserve our health and strength; and when we abstain from taking too much or too rich food or drink. We also practise temperance when we keep our passions under due restraint; when especially we duly moderate our anger, and refrain from hatred and revenge; when we dress and live well within our means; and when, in general, we confine our pleasures to acts which are then and there good and useful and therefore lawful.

309. The Eight Beatitudes (Mat. v. 3—10). These are Christ's Commandments to His elect.

They are Commandments each " with a promise."

They are thus the Gospel of God in short, the " glad tidings" brought us by the " orient from on high."

" Blessed are the poor in spirit "—those that in poverty are contented in it; those that in wealth use it not for themselves but for the glory of God and the succour of God's little ones; those especially that give up all to follow Christ—" for theirs is the kingdom of heaven."

" Blessed are the meek "—those that return good for evil, that forgive injuries, that pray for their calumniators and enemies—" for they shall possess the land."

" Blessed are they that mourn "—that grieve for sin, that deplore the injury they and others have done to God—" for they shall be comforted."

" Blessed are they that hunger and thirst after righteousness "—who long not for pleasure or earthly gain, but long to be better and better, to " go from virtue unto virtue," to " be justified still," and " be sanctified still " further—" for they shall be filled " (with the righteousness they long for).

" Blessed are the merciful "—that show compassion to the frail, the faltering, the suffering, and the poor; that do the works of mercy, corporal and spiritual—" for they shall obtain mercy."

"Blessed are the clean of heart"—they that love holy purity; they that are chaste in body and chaste in soul; they that are virgins in will as well as in act—"for they shall see God."

"Blessed are the peace-makers"—they that love the peace of God; they that lead men to peace by leading them to truth; they that make men to be at peace with God and at peace with each other—"for they shall be called the children of God."

"Blessed are they that suffer persecution for righteousness sake"—that follow truth, obey the Faith, refuse to sin, and are, therefore, persecuted by the wicked—"for theirs is the kingdom of heaven."

These Beatitudes, then, are so many modes of practising Charity or love towards God; so many calls to perfection; so many commandments to those to whom God's merest wish is law; so many paths towards heaven; so many promises and pledges of future glory, because so many means of actually foretasting here below the joy and the blessedness of heaven, as the experience of the saints has abundantly proved.

310. The Works of Mercy.—As followers of Christ we are called upon, according to our means and opportunities:—

    To feed the hungry,
    To give drink to the thirsty,
    To clothe the naked,
    To harbour the harbourless,
    To visit the sick,
    To visit the imprisoned,
    To bury the dead;
And also—
    To bring sinners to repentance,
    To instruct the ignorant,
    To counsel the doubtful,
    To comfort the sorrowful,
    To bear wrongs patiently,

To forgive injuries,
And to pray for the living and the dead.

Not the priest alone, or the sister of charity, but every Christian in his measure, is called upon to act in the person of Christ, and to perform some one or more of these corporal or spiritual Works of Mercy.

311. The Evangelical Counsels, or Gospel Recommendations.—These are Voluntary Poverty, Perpetual Chastity, and Entire Obedience.

A person living in the world may, if he feel that he has the call from God, "sell all that he has and give to the poor;" he may resolve never to marry, and offer his virginity as a perpetual sacrifice to God; and he may put himself under obedience, in all things lawful, to one who has no right or claim to command him.

These things a man or woman may do, in imitation and in love of Christ, to serve God the better, even living in the world.

Or, better still, such a one may join a religious order, and bind himself by vows, to serve God until death in these more excellent ways.

312. The Fruits of the Spirit.—"The fruit of the Spirit," says St. Paul, "is Charity, joy, peace, patience, benignity, goodness, longanimity, mildness, faith, modesty, continency, chastity" (Gal. v. 22).

And, again, he describes Charity thus: "Charity is patient, is kind; charity envieth not, dealeth not perversely, is not puffed up, is not ambitious, seeketh not her own, is not provoked to anger, thinketh no evil, rejoiceth not in iniquity, but rejoiceth with the truth: beareth all things, believeth all things, hopeth all things, endureth all things. Charity never falleth away" (1 Cor. xiii. 4—8).

All this, then, we are called to be, and to show forth in our lives and actions.

If this is our character we are Christians indeed, and the Spirit of God has not been given to us in vain.

But if we are not all this, then have we more to learn, more to do, more to aim at, more to pray for.

Let us, therefore, examine ourselves and see ; for the time is short, and " He that giveth testimony of these things saith, Surely I come quickly. Amen" (Apoc. xxii. 20).

313. Conclusion.—These, then, are the First Lessons in Christianity.

Good and evil have now been set forth as explained by our Lord Jesus Christ Himself—the evil that you may avoid it, the good that you may do it.

And these things indeed are the beginnings of Christianity.

For the Church has boundless treasures of wisdom laid up in the Holy Scriptures, in the books of Mystical and Ascetical Theology, and in the writings, meditations and revelations of the Saints.

And a soul that lays well the foundations of Faith and Charity may be led by the Spirit of God to the knowledge of things higher and higher—mysteries of Providence—which it is scarcely given to man to utter.

Declaration.—All that is written in this little book has been written to explain the old " Faith once delivered to the Saints." All is hereby submitted for correction or approval to the proper ecclesiastical authorities ; especially to the holy Roman See, which alone has the plenitude of power and knowledge to judge of all teaching, and from whose decision there is no appeal.

THE END.

INDEX.

A

	PAGE.
ABSOLUTION	147
Abstinence	175
Acts of Faith, Hope, Charity	79
Actual Graces	55
Adoration	81
Agnosticism	83
Altar and the Cross	128
Angels	13, 14
Apostasy	84
Apostles' Creed	10
Ascension	25
Atheism	83
Attributes, of God	11

B

BANNS	162
Baptism	108—117
Beatitudes	184
Birth of our Redeemer	19
Brotherly Love	76

C

CALUMNY	104
Cardinal Virtues, Practice of	182
Celibacy of Clergy	156
Ceremonies, Use of	171
Charity	72—77
Children, Duties and Sins of	92
Christian Church	4
Christian Religion	3
Church, The Catholic	29—46
,, Members of	42
,, Militant	42
,, Notes of	33—35
,, Other Properties of	35
,, Suffering	43
,, Teaching	29
,, Triumphant	43
Commandments	78—106

C

	PAGE
Communion, Holy	132—136
,, in one kind	132
,, Spiritual	134
Communion of Saints	44—46
Confessing the Faith	80
Confession	140—142
,, Utility of	142
,, Seal or Secrecy of	143
Confirmation	117—120
Conquering of sin	179
Contrition	157
Converts, Reception of	116
Creator, God the	13
Creeds	41

D

DEALING WITH THE DEVIL	85
Deism	86
Despair	84
Detraction	104
Divinity of Jesus Christ	16
Duelling	91
Dying, How to help the	153

E

EARTH AND MAN	14
End of world	61
Eucharist, The Holy	121—131
Evangelical counsels	183
Expectation of Messias	5
Extreme Unction	149—152

F

FAITH	7
Fasting	175
,, Object and institution of	176

F

	PAGE.
False religions	8
Forgiveness of sins	46, 50,
,, Conditions of	48
Forgiver, God the-	47
Free will	15
Fruits of Holy Mass	130
Fruits of the Spirit	187

G

GIFTS OF THE SPIRIT	54
God and the soul	1
Godfather and Godmother	110
Good works	55

H

"HAIL MARY," THE	70
Heaven	13
Heresy	83
Holy Ghost	27
,, Gift of	51
,, Twofold office of	28
,, Work in the Church	28
,, Work in the soul	29
Holy Order	154—158
Holy Water	172
Hope	63
How to marry well	164
Humanity of Christ	20
Husband and wife, Duties of	95
Hypostatic Union	20

I

IDOLATRY	85
Ignorance	84
Immaculate Conception	18
Impediments to marriage	160
Impurity	100
Incarnation	19
Indulgencies	58
Infalibility of Church	35
,, of Pope	32
Infused Virtues	54
Intercessory Prayer	67
Invocation of Saints	67

J

JESUS CHRIST	3
Judaism	83

J

	PAGE.
Justification	50
,, What it does not do	60
Judgment	61, 62

L

LIFE EVERLASTING	62
Likeness of God in Soul	15
Lucifer	13
Lying	108

M

MAHOMETANISM	83
Marriage Service	166
Mass	127—132
,, How to hear	131
,, Obligation of Hearing	91
Matrimony	158—167
Matter and Form of Sacraments	168
Mediator, Christ the One	27
Meditation	71
Melchisedech	126
Merit	56
Miracles of Christ	21
Mixed Marriages	168
Murder	97

N

Names of Christ	26
Nature of Man	14
Nuptial Mass	166

O

Oaths	87—89
Obligation of Christians	178
Orders, Sacred	155
Ordination, Conditions for	158
"Our Father," The	69

P

PARENTS, DUTIES OF	93
Passion and death of Christ	22
Penance, Sacrament of	136—149
,, or satisfaction	146

P

	PAGE
Prayer	63—71
,, Power of	59
Precepts of the Church	174—178
Presumption	84
Primacy of St. Peter	30
,, perpetual	32
,, Effects of	32
Punishments due to sin	17, 57

R

REAL PRESENCE	124
Relics	82
Religion, Virtue of	80
Repentance	137, 140
Restitution, for theft	102
,, for calumny	104
Resurrection	25
Revelation	2
,, Completion of	36
Righteousness of God	52
Rising of the dead	62

S

SABBATH	89
Sacramentals	172—174
Sacraments	37, 108
,, General doctrine of	167—171
Sacrifice	22
,, of Cross	24
,, of Mass	127
Sacrifices of Old Law	23
Sacrilege	86
Sanctifying Grace	52
Satisfaction	58
Saviour, Promise of	18
Scandal	99
Scripture	38
,, Utility of	38
,, Insufficiency of, as a rule of faith	40
,, Interpretation of	40
Second coming of Christ	27, 61
Servants	96
Servile work	90
Shechinah	52
Sick, Recommendations about	154
Sign of the Cross	173
Simony	86
Sin of Adam	15
Sin, Actual	16, 47
,, Mortal	16

S

Sin, Original	16, 47
,, Venial	17
Sponsors in Baptism	110
,, in Confirmation	120
Stealing	101
Summary of Tenth Art. of Creed	59
Superstition	86
Superiors and their subjects, Duties and sins of	95—97

T

TEACHING OF CHRIST	21
Temporal Punishment	57
Temptations	107
,, How to conquer	107
Testament, Old and New	5
,, New, Utility of	38
Theological Virtues, Practice of	181
Thoughts, Evil	106
Tradition	36
,, Instruments of	37—42
Transubstantiation	128
Trinity	12
True Religion	9

U

Usury	102

V

Viaticum	136
Vocation	157
Vows	87—89

W

Way of Perfection	181
Way of Salvation	6
Working out of Salvation	179
Works of Mercy	185
Worship, Degrees of	82
Worship due to Christ	26
Worship of Mary	82
Worship of Relics and Images	82
Worship of Saints	81

www.ingramcontent.com/pod-product-compliance
Lightning Source LLC
Chambersburg PA
CBHW020840160426
43192CB00007B/731